Job Reconnaissance

Job Reconnaissance

Using Hacking Skills to Win the Job Hunt Game

Josh More

Edited by
Beth Friedman

AMSTERDAM • BOSTON • HEIDELBERG • LONDON
NEW YORK • OXFORD • PARIS • SAN DIEGO
SAN FRANCISCO • SINGAPORE • SYDNEY • TOKYO

ELSEVIER

Syngress is an imprint of Elsevier

SYNGRESS.

Elsevier
The Boulevard, Langford Lane, Kidlington, Oxford, OX5 1GB, UK
225 Wyman Street, Waltham, MA 02451, USA

First published 2014

Notices
Knowledge and best practice in this field are constantly changing. As new research and experience broaden our understanding, changes in research methods, professional practices, or medical treatment may become necessary.

Practitioners and researchers must always rely on their own experience and knowledge in evaluating and using any information, methods, compounds, or experiments described herein. In using such information or methods they should be mindful of their own safety and the safety of others, including parties for whom they have a professional responsibility.

To the fullest extent of the law, neither the Publisher nor the authors, contributors, or editors, assume any liability for any injury and/or damage to persons or property as a matter of products liability, negligence or otherwise, or from any use or operation of any methods, products, instructions, or ideas contained in the material herein.

British Library Cataloguing in Publication Data
A catalogue record for this book is available from the British Library

Library of Congress Cataloging-in-Publication Data
A catalog record for this book is available from the Library of Congress

ISBN: 978-0-12-416601-1

For information on all Syngress publications
visit our website at store.elsevier.com/syngress

This book has been manufactured using Print On Demand technology. Each copy is produced to order and is limited to black ink. The online version of this book will show color figures where appropriate.

Working together
to grow libraries in
developing countries

www.elsevier.com • www.bookaid.org

CONTENTS

ACKNOWLEDGMENTS

This book evolved out of a very long process originating back in 2004, when I pursued my first job found with this process. The journey included finding the job after that and helping several friends find jobs of their own. Along the way, it became two different presentations and one fairly popular blog post. So, first and foremost, this book could not exist without a conversation stretching across almost a decade with a great many people.

In particular, though, I would like to thank Beth Friedman, my copyeditor on this book. Beth drastically improved my language here, so if this book is readable, thank her.

This book involves many issues that could be considered marginally ethical, so I would very much like to thank my beta readers. This book was made significantly better because of the contributions of the information security community, specifically those of Wes Earnest, David Matusiak, Peter Nikolaidis, Michael Rogers, Armond Rouillard, Hord Tipton, Shawna Turner-Rice, and Kris Wicks. These people were able to point out many ethical concerns that I had missed in the first draft, so thanks definitely go out to them.

I would also like to thank my beta readers outside of the information security community: Martin Demello, David Dyer-Bennet, Fred Levy Haskell, and David McLaughlin. There were many others, too numerous to list here, who read the book in partial forms or helped me with the original presentations. Some of their work is listed in the Resources section at the end of this book.

Finally, all graphics in this book were made with the open source tools LibreOffice, Inkscape, and The Gimp. A big thank-you goes out to the multitude of programmers who volunteered years of development to make these tools what they are and to release them for free for everyone.

You are about to read a book on job hunting, but it's not your usual sort of book.

The usual sorts will teach you individual skills—how to identify what you want to do, how to craft résumés, how to dress, how to interview well, how to negotiate for salary, etc. This book is different. It will teach you a process for *getting* not just a job, but a job that will make you happy and make you feel fulfilled—for a long time. This book will touch on the individual skills in passing, but it's the *process* that's important, and that's what this book is about.

This book is not intended to stand alone. Many people already own other job hunting books. This book is a supplement—a patch, if you will—to areas that other books tend not to cover well. You will not find detailed strategies on how to answer interview questions or engage in salary negotiations. You will, however, find a detailed process to discover and use information about prospective companies and the people there. The fundamental thesis behind this approach is that foreknowledge is better than learning after the fact. Anything you can learn ahead of time could save you a catastrophic failure in the interview process, so this book is about information. It's about reconnaissance.

THE ETHICS OF RECONNAISSANCE AND JOB SEARCHING

Reconnaissance techniques have been developed over centuries. They have been widely used by military forces identifying what the enemy was doing, police forces tracking criminals and potential criminals, spies looking into the actions of other countries, private detectives (and governments) monitoring private citizens, and now, with the Internet, by everyone. As these techniques have been developed and honed, an ethical framework has evolved around them. The more you learn about a person, the more power you have over them. A secret that gets out may have the power to destroy a marriage, someone's savings, or even a life. Information shared with a private group, but with the wrong privacy settings, can reveal information that the person would much prefer to stay secret. You must choose where you stand on this issue. Just because the information is available doesn't mean that it is right for you to use it.

This book presumes that you are a mature, trustworthy adult who is passingly familiar with your local and national laws. You can certainly choose to abuse the tools and techniques in this book and manipulate situations to your advantage. However, bear in mind that (as pointed out by Spider-Man) with great power comes great responsibility. One trick is to try to reverse the situation and see how you'd feel if the information you found applied to you ...though you might be smart enough to not post your family information on a church mailing list and your bedroom practices with your lover on a fetish site, not everyone is quite so wise. Even the most innocuous sharing of data can have significant implications. A church mailing list can reveal names, birth dates, and addresses of individuals. Ads on sites like Craigslist and photos uploaded to the web can uncover physical locations, and social networks like Facebook and Twitter can help you discover social relationships. As you go through the process, filter out information that isn't pertinent to the job-hunting process itself and try to respect the privacy of those you are investigating.

The benefits of following this process can be huge, but the costs if you are caught misusing someone's personal information can be extremely high. This extends beyond the simple consequence of failing to get the job; it could involve legal costs, being blacklisted, or, in extreme situations, jail time. By protecting your targets you will protect yourself.

●●●──

Public Sector Work

If you are leaving a public sector job (government or military) and looking to join the private sector, many of these suggestions may make you quite uncomfortable. On one hand, the rules are different. The private sector is considerably more lax, and some organizations take an "anything goes" approach. However, this varies by industry. In general, the invisible line between right and wrong tends to move around. A rule of thumb is that the older an industry is, the closer that line will be to what you're used to. Banks, for example, will follow a similar code of ethics as governments and militaries. Information technology start-up firms, however, will tend play fast and loose. Before you go any further, think about where the ethical lines are for the industries you are targeting and whether you'd be comfortable playing by those rules. Realize that people competing with you for those jobs will be playing by those rules and that if you choose to work off of a more restrictive set of ethical guidelines, you'll be putting yourself at a disadvantage. There's nothing wrong with that, but it will make your life more difficult.

If you are in the opposite situation, coming from the private sector (or no sector) and considering a job in the public sector, know that the rules will be tight and much of what's in this book could work against you. If you do not have experience in that area, find someone who does and run your plan past them. They should be able to point out any red flags in what you're thinking about doing and may be able to help you decide whether or not you even want to work in that sort of environment.

Like reconnaissance, people have been engaging in job searches for quite a long time. It is tempting to believe that it is acceptable to lie on your résumé and overhype things you've done in the past. There is a general belief that "everyone does it," so you might as well.

However, reconnaissance runs in two directions. Just as you can find out information about prospective employers, they can discover information about you. If you lie, you will be found out. Stories abound where exaggerations on résumés land the job, and then land the job seeker in hot water. In a world where everything you do is stored on the Internet forever, mistakes can follow you for your entire life. If you make up a certification that you don't have, fabricate work history, or claim to have a skill you've not developed, not only is it wrong, but when caught, it could end your career.

Even following your own ethics could have this result, as individuals such as Chelsea Manning and Edward Snowden have discovered. This is a book about the "big picture" and how, to succeed, you must work in conjunction with others. Just as their actions affect you, your actions affect them. There is no guarantee that acting ethically with respect to the job search process will keep you out of trouble, but it's a lot less likely to cause you harm than acting unethically will.

THE COLD, HARD TRUTH

There are many types of books on job hunting. Many of them start simply and make the process seem straightforward. There are good reasons for that approach. Being without a job can be emotionally difficult, and it's easy to give up. By trying to smooth over such emotional issues, it can be easier to help the reader. If it helps them get a job faster, the reader will recommend the book when someone else needs a new job.

This book, by necessity, takes a different approach. The core concept behind this approach to the job search is that by understanding the economics that affect the organizations you target for jobs and the psychology of those hiring, you can maximize your chances for success. Sadly, however, economics and psychology are something of downer topics. There's a reason economics is often called "the dismal science." If you find yourself in a temporary slump, check Appendix C, get yourself unstuck, then resume following the process.

There are four cold, hard truths to employment. No one will give you a job because you're nice. No one will give you a job because you're smart. You do not have a right to a job. The only reason anyone will give you a job worth doing is because you will make them more money than you will cost.

This is how economics works. Someone in power, often a business owner, makes a bet that employing you will benefit them more than it will cost them. You are hired to reduce someone's pain or increase someone's money. That's it. Drop all expectations that the process is about you. It's not. It's about them. In fact, the more you think about this fact, the better off you'll do for yourself. Keeping in mind how others will view you will help to keep your message clean, simple, and focused on their needs.

If you understand that you are just a cog in a vast machine consisting of people working together to make a very small number of people very, very rich, you become better able to do your part to make those people very, very rich. The better you get at this, the more of their money they'll let you have.

It's sad, but the world can be hard and cruel. However, in a hard and cruel world, the time you spend bemoaning your fate is time that others are using to get one up on you. All you can manage is your own time and financial resources. By using these effectively, and magnifying your effectiveness with your own knowledge, you can take control of your own life.

That's what this process is about. Some of the advice in this book can be interpreted as manipulative or mean. That is because, at its root, it is. You do not have to follow all of the advice herein. If anything makes you uncomfortable, feel free to skip it. However, before you skip anything, think about the pros and cons and make an informed decision. Keep in mind that this book builds upon itself, so you may wish to read the entire book before making this decision.

GEEK CULTURE

This book is written primarily for introverts—for people who are more comfortable sitting behind a computer screen than getting out and talking to people. If you are one of those people, odds are that your previous job searches consisted of sending out dozens of résumés to hundreds of organizations or posting them in online job boards in the hope that someone who read one of them would deign to give you an interview. Then, once you got that interview, you were nervous and tongue-tied and muddled your way through as best you could. You may be a hard worker, you may be brilliant and creative, but odds are that you constantly play second fiddle to extroverted people who aren't as skilled as you at anything but talking with other people. It's human nature to value people who can talk well.

Face it—you are not going to develop powerful social skills overnight. If you thought you could, you'd be reading a different book, possibly one written by Stephen Covey or Anthony Robbins. Odds are that what you'd really like is a technical solution to a social problem. Sadly, you're not going to get one here. This book will provide the next best thing. What you are going to get is a process that can be followed to help you use your technical skills to make you stand out. You will still need decent social skills, but they needn't be stellar. You do not have to be a scintillating conversationalist to land a job. You just need to be good enough to avoid sabotaging yourself as you let your technical skills work their magic.

This book is about focusing on your strengths. You might be great at discovering information, detail work, document layout, or at seeing the big picture. Focus there, but make sure that the other skills the process will require of you (research, planning, writing, negotiation, etc.) are good enough that you can handle the situation facing you.

This book is about playing a "long game." At some point, you will find that it becomes harder and harder to find a job at "the next level," where you get more money, more joy, or more meaning out of the work you do. The economics of the employment market drive employers to hire people who have already proven they can do the job the employer is hiring for, so the levels, such as they are, become less flexible over time, and it gets easier and easier to get stuck. By following the process described herein, you will slowly gain the skills you need to push into a new role. The long game takes a while to get started, but once you start playing it, you'll find that the barriers in your way begin to drop away.

Simply following the process will not make your job search fair. It will, however, help to level the playing field against your less technical but more social competition.

PROTECTION AND AVOIDANCE

Almost every book about job hunting discusses the issues of illegal questions and discrimination. This can involve issues of race, gender, age, family situation, legalities involving multiple countries, and so on. With a few minor exceptions, this book ignores the issue entirely. The goal of the process is to wow your interviewers with your excellence, not to play it safe hiding behind legal protection. The laws preventing interviewers from asking questions about your race, gender, sexual orientation, and family plans exist for a reason, and there are predatory employers out there. Some people only interview as a formality, but their hiring practices show sexist, racist, ableist, and ageist views. These laws exist to limit the ability of people in positions of power from egregiously abusing their power.

Such legal protection is vital in traditional avenues towards hiring. However, the entire point of this book is to recognize that traditional avenues are starting to fail, and the balance of power may be shifted more towards you, the job seeker. If you manage to adapt to the new paradigm and become an early adopter, the game changes drastically. Just as employers can become predatory and take advantage of their power, it is possible for you to do the same and become a predatory job seeker. Some of the techniques discussed herein can be used to bribe, bully, or blackmail your way into employment. However, just as predatory hiring techniques seldom result in valuable employees, predatory job seeking seldom results in useful and enjoyable work.

Instead, the goal of this process is to identify that both you and the organization you target will be better off together than separate. In other words, you want to get your interviewers to fall in love with you, and you cannot do this by hiding who you are.

By the time you get to an interview, you will be stereotyped. There's nothing you can do to avoid this. Your age, whether too young or too old, will be held against you. What gender you present as will be a factor. Accents and modes of speaking will say something about your class and upbringing. Your skin tone and facial features will be used to draw conclusions about you. All this is true: unfair, but true.

However, there's not a single thing you can do about this, and a job interview is seldom the right place to fight institutional discrimination. If you are interviewing with such a person, recognize that and think about whether you want the job enough to deal with that level of misconception and abuse. It is quite possible to work with a racist or sexist boss and still have an overall positive experience. There's nothing wrong with viewing this job as a stepping-stone to gain the skills to go somewhere else eventually. As with many things, your career is a journey and some parts will be less than perfect. However, if you think you have the skills to do better, feel free to stop focusing on your target at any time and look to apply the process to a better opportunity.

HOW TO READ THIS BOOK

This book is process-based. You may not need every chapter. You may not need every piece of advice in each chapter. However, the process as a whole is one that has been used for generations. The only difference is that this book takes the Internet into consideration and equips you with vast amounts of data to maximize your success. Read the table of contents to get a feel for the overall process flow. Then skim each chapter to make sure you understand how it all works together. At that point, feel free to read the entire book or just the pieces you need.

The process is highly flexible, but it works best when you are flexible as well.

CHAPTER 1

Foundations: What You Ought to Have Done before Buying This Book

Before you begin looking for a job, there are some things you should already have done. Granted, most people don't pick up books like this unless they're already on the market, so if you have to move faster than ideal, feel free to skim the book and only read and execute on the chapters that directly apply to you. However, keep in mind that the stronger a foundation you can establish for yourself, the faster you'll be able to springboard off of it.

This foundation will consist of an assortment of online presences such as websites, blogs, and microblogs. It may include public-facing documents (papers, presentations, articles, books, etc.) that you have put together to demonstrate your abilities. All of this together can help back you up as you go through the rest of the process.

If you have not established a firm foundation, many of your job-seeking efforts will fail, even if you're doing all the right things. So before you start targeting firms, read through this chapter and map out what you do and do not do well. Then, as you work the process, begin filling in your gaps. You can also use this process to find alternative activities that may provide a break from the stresses of job hunting without your having to give up forward progress.

TASK MANAGEMENT

Each section in this chapter focuses on things you should, ideally, have been doing for the last several years. Odds are you weren't doing many of them, if any. It can feel overwhelming to look at a list like this. You may already be emotionally shaken because you lost a job or are trapped in one that's bad for you. So as you read this, remember that daily progress towards your primary goal, finding a new job, comes first. Important things are seldom accomplished in one go. Marathons take weeks of training, books take months to write, and cathedrals take generations to build. The key is to keep going, a little bit at a time, every day.

For this process to work, you must have a goal in mind. It is likely that this goal will shift as you read this book. That's fine. As people grow and change, so does what they want out of life. The important thing is to know what the goal is, whether it's to find a new job with better money, more comfortable working culture, increased flexibility, or something else. If you know what your goal is, you stand a much better chance of achieving it, one piece at a time.

If thinking about doing all of these things causes you to stall out or shut down, the set is not worth doing—at least, not in its entirety. Consider, instead, working on a single piece of the project. This could involve making a single public-facing document. It could be an adjustment to your website. Things that seem impossible to do in their entirety are often much less intimidating to do one step at a time.

TIME MANAGEMENT

This is not a book on time management. If you need one, please check Appendix A. However, there are some tips that have worked very well for other people. Running a job search is just like running a project—but unlike a project, you are both the one providing the service and the client. Success is dependent on maintaining progress, but the progress must be towards your goal. Any task that does not move you towards your goal should be removed from your list. It is far too easy to lose time doing things that are easy and open-ended but provide little to no value.

When managing your time, it helps to have a list of tasks. Many people find that this system works best when the list of tasks is fully known. After all, the more complete the list is, the less likely you are to get stressed over remembering things that should be on the list. However, the more complete your list, the more overwhelming it can seem. This is why multiple lists are important. Consider maintaining lists for things like:

- Things to do today
- Things to do this week

- Things that are blocked (by someone else, by another task, by scheduling, etc.)
- Things that just won't get done this week
- Things that just won't get done anytime soon
- Things that recur periodically

Then, before you do something that doesn't move you towards your goal, check your "Things to do today" list and verify that you've made enough progress towards your goals that slacking off a bit isn't going to hurt you more than it helps. The issue here is that it's easy to have a "down" day, especially if you are job hunting. When you have such a day, it's easy to have "take an hour off" turn into "take a day off," which can stretch into a few days, and before you know it, an entire week has gone by with no progress made. By putting the list of tasks first on such days, you can select an item that doesn't take much energy, so you can push yourself to progress towards your goal even on days when you really don't want to.

More information on specific ways to manage your tasks can be found in the Resources section at the end of this book. Fundamentally, though, you have to remember to take care of yourself. Human bodies have needs. You will make steadier and more rapid progress towards your goal if you eat in a healthy manner, sleep well, and get exercise. You probably don't need to be reminded of this, but it is extremely easy to forget. There are two common scenarios you face in the job search. Either you've lost your job and you're looking for a new one or you have a job you don't like and you're looking for a new one.

These two scenarios come with different stressors. If you've lost your job, you'll be short on money but long on time. If you have a job and are looking for a new one at the same time, you'll be short on time but (comparatively) long on money.

Anything that causes you to fritter away your scant resources could result in your not taking care of yourself, your resources, and your goals. If you have no job and are stressing out, a night on the town might feel like a good stress reliever. However, if after that night out, you're a few hundred dollars shorter, those are dollars you can't use to move yourself forward. If you're stressed from job hunting and working 40−60 hours per week, and feel like sitting down to watch a new season of TV, you can lose 24 hours of your life without noticing it. You can't get this time back, and realizing that you failed to make progress on your job search could add more stress than the downtime relieved.

That's not to say that you can't take breaks. Breaks are essential. Just don't take breaks in a way that will harm you more than they will help.

Finally, finding a new job requires managing a lot of data. This is also not a book on data management. For specific pointers to other places to learn this skill, please see the Resources section. That said, in general, simpler systems work better. People who try to put everything into a database often wind up spending more time playing with the data system than actually using the data. Whether you work best with text files, wikis, mind mappers, spreadsheets, or just plain old pen and paper, choose one and use the system as best you can. Tweaking data management systems is fun but can be an amazing time sink, since it's never completely finished. This time sink is, in fact, one of the most dangerous risks to the job search process. So before you start a task, determine what "done" looks like.

Whether you are analyzing and improving your data, researching companies, or working on documentation, any open-ended task may be more appealing to you than something more concrete. After all, once you finish the discrete task, you'll have to start something new, possibly something that you don't want to do at all (which is why you're procrastinating on open-ended tasks). So before you start any-thing, get a clear idea in your mind what the completed task should look like. If you find it difficult to do this, then decide how much time it is worth to you and set a timer. When the timer goes off, you've reached "done," at least for now, and it's time to move on to some-thing else that moves you towards your goal.

With that, assuming your time and data management systems are ready to go, there are some basic things you should have in place before you can massively succeed at the job hunt.

YOUR PERSONAL BRAND

Your personal brand is, to drastically simplify things, a mixture of who you are, who you project yourself to be, and who other people think you are. The better these three things match one another, the stronger your brand is.

Why does this matter?

There are two ways to get a job. The first is to submit your résumé plus a cover letter to a bunch of companies over and over again in the hopes that someday they'll pick you. Then, when you get into the job, you get to hope it's a good fit for you so you're not right back in the same situation next year.

There is another way to get a job, and that is what this book is about. Basically, instead of trying to get a company to choose you, you choose the company. This is a slower but more active process. However, when you succeed at this process, you will be happier in the eventual job. This is because by helping the company create a job that fits you, more of your time will be spent doing what you want to do.

The company will be creating a job that blends its needs with what it perceives your needs to be. Thus, the closer the persona that you convey in an interview is to the person you truly are (or want to become), the more closely the eventual job will fit you as you grow. Many people leave jobs because they grow beyond them. Other people wind up in a job they dislike because, in the interview, they pretended to be someone other than who they truly are. By keeping this in mind and understanding what you really want, you'll be in a good position to thrive once you get into the job.

That means you first have to understand who you are and what you want. Only then can you work on how you convey yourself and appear to others. Then, as time goes by and you project this version of yourself over and over again, you gradually start to become that person, and the perceptions of others slowly start to merge with that identity as well.

This sounds like a strong claim to make, but it's been true even since Shakespeare's time: "Assume a virtue if you have it not ... for use can almost change the stamp of nature."

So that's the theory. What's the practice?

Website
You have a website, right? A real website with a dedicated domain name and everything. Not https://www.facebook.com/hornyone, https://www.

facebook.com/hottotrot, or https://www.facebook.com/stoner. (These are all real profiles at the time of this writing.)

Your website should exist, look professional, and convey at a glance who you are. The domain name you choose should be, at the very least, non-objectionable. When you start contacting people as you follow this process, they're going to infer your website address from your email address and check out your site. The site doesn't have to be robust, but it does have to be complete.

Your website should have, at a minimum, your résumé, some of the documents described below, and a way to contact you. Whether you put your photo on your site is entirely up to you. In general, it helps, but there are situations where it can hurt you. White males, for example, don't face much discrimination. This is not true for everyone. If you feel that you may be discriminated against for what others assume from your photograph, you may not wish to put it online. That said, if they're going to discriminate against you, the job wouldn't be a good fit anyway, so you might want to use the photo anyway since it could help you filter out companies that would be bad for you.

You may also wish to flesh out your website with information about you as a person. As you do this, put a spin on any hobbies you have, so they apply at least somewhat peripherally to your industry. The more you can look like an interesting and well-rounded person, the more you'll stand out from the crowd. The more consistent a story you tell about yourself, the better you will be able to "click" with the people interviewing you. A few good rules of thumb for deciding what to put online for professional branding:

- If the activity is a hobby for a majority of people, don't bother; you won't stand out. "I like to watch football on Sundays" isn't going to help you get hired. "I like to volunteer at the library and read to kids" just might.
- If the activity is viewed negatively within your target industry, either avoid it entirely or find a way to tweak it to show how it applies. "I collect tattoos of penguins" is very different from "I like to experiment with Linux and keep track of the distributions I've used."
- Visual hobbies work better online than nonvisual ones. Consider two websites, one with collections of interesting photos from trips

all over the world and one with collections of philosophical tracts exploring the nature of death. They're both quite interesting in their own right, but only one is likely to result in a reaction of "I want to meet this person."

- Things that are amusing work well so long as the humor is clean, accessible, and non-offensive. It makes you seem more appealing, and it also means that as more and more people link to your site, it will rank higher in the search engines. More of this will be discussed in the search engine optimization section.
- As you spin your hobbies, look for ways that you can discuss them while showing off critical thinking and analysis skills, writing skills, and creativity.

LinkedIn

You should have a LinkedIn profile of some sort. Most organizations doing hiring these days will check you out there. They might not refer to any other site, but they'll check LinkedIn. So if you don't have an account, create one. If you do have one, do a quick check of how your profile is set up. You must have a profile that quickly describes who you are. You should have some form of work history listed. Consider also adding a photo, but only if it is professional in nature—you should appear well-groomed and be dressed professionally. If you don't have one of those, get a friend to take some of you and choose one to post. Almost any head shot looks decent when shrunk down to icon size. Make sure the background is clean and that you're smiling. If you are a member of a minority group and fear discrimination, consider skipping the photo—but also consider that if you're going to get discriminated against based on how you look, is it really worth putting forth all the effort necessary to land the interview?

Then, while you're at the LinkedIn site, check out some groups and consider joining conversations there. Connect to enough people to make it look as though you're active in a community. A reasonable goal would be to find 50 or so people on LinkedIn willing to link to you. More is better, of course, but try to select people who have something to do with your field of expertise. A profile with nothing but family and recruiters looks suspicious. If possible, try to connect with senior-level people. Those listed as director, vice president, and titles starting with a "C" will make you look more impressive.

If you are on good terms with some of the people to whom you are linked, consider asking them for recommendations and endorsements. How much these work in your favor will depend on the person reviewing your profile, but they are unlikely to harm you. If you don't want your boss to find out you're looking, consider soliciting recommendations from bosses, coworkers, and customers that you have worked with in the past but that are no longer affiliated with your current employer.

Finally, open up your privacy settings a bit to make sure that prospective employers can see your profile and contact you. Yes, this does involve a bit of risk, but it is far outweighed by the potential rewards. If unexpected potential employers contact you, it's a chance to practice your skills. If people reach out to you with technical questions, you can begin building an online reputation. Then, as your network grows, you not only look more impressive to prospective employers but you also develop a set of people to whom you can reach out for assistance.

Blog

It's important to show what you think. It is also important to convey the fact that you can communicate with others. Blogs are excellent for this. You can either combine your blog and your website or keep them separate. Which method you choose depends on your skill level, but really, this is up to you. The important thing is to have a place where people can read your takes on several different issues.

If you've been blogging for the last five years, that's great. All you probably have to do is polish things up a bit and make sure that nothing in poor taste still exists out there. If you have *not* been blogging, it's time to start. Fortunately, most blogs allow you to back date entries. Get your feet wet in the past. Keep past articles relatively generic, and aim for one post per historical month to get you caught up to today. A full year catch-up would mean 12 to 24 different posts, which isn't all that much. Additionally, by the time you've done those, you'll be able to churn out posts on current events quickly and, along the process, you'll be more likely to have found your own voice so posts will sound more self-consistent.

Besides, you shouldn't think of them as over 20 things you have to write. Think of them, instead, as 20 job ads you're putting up, for free, all talking about how cool you are.

A warning is needed here. While the general approach of this book is to let you, the reader, determine what is and isn't ethical in your situation, creating content can be tricky. If you're targeting a specific company, learning what they need and creating content around that need is fine. Backdating that content might be fine. However, the further back you go, the greater a risk you take in being detected ... and you *can* be detected.

Also, backdating content to such an extent that you are effectively creating a fraudulent work history is almost always going to get you into trouble. In much the same way that you shouldn't lie on your résumé, you shouldn't create an implicit lie as you generate content. Write about what you've learned and what you've done, by all means. Don't write about things you've never done, and don't reuse someone else's work without giving them credit. All the work you do, whether it's for hire or not, should be able to stand on its own merits. If it can't do that, work a bit harder and learn a bit more until it can.

Microblogs, Social Platforms, and Forums
Microblogs like Twitter, social platforms like Facebook, and forums like LinkedIn Discussions can be good ways to get your name out there. However, they can also be amazing time sinks. If you are not already using communication platforms like these, they may not be worth joining. People can tell when you're just networking to get a job, and you just won't get much return on investment that way. If, however, you've been on these sites for a while, you should leverage them to your advantage.

If there is no risk to your current job (assuming you are employed) from letting people know you're looking, make sure that the most popular people in your online groups know you're looking. Don't ask them for anything, just occasionally mention what you're looking for in areas that they'll notice. Highly networked people notice things like that automatically, and even if they don't respond, they know. When they see someone looking for what you can provide, they'll connect you.

Also, make sure your forum postings contain a signature that links back to your website. This will boost your search ranking and make it easier for prospective employers to check you out—so make sure you use relatively professional language. Anything you do online should be considered public, because you never know when a site's privacy controls are going to fail or change. To make yourself look more engaged, create a list of links that you can mine on a regular basis. As this process continues, you will be finding and reading all sorts of interesting things about your industry. At least three times per week, you should post one of those links with a short comment to your microblog sites. At minimum, this should be on Twitter and LinkedIn, but consider other sharing sites as well if you find that any of your targeted people have social presences there. As you do this, be sure to comment only on what you actually know. Name recognition goes both ways, and not all attention is positive. It doesn't take all that much time to verify what you have to say before you say it, so take the time.

CONTENT CREATION

Once you've built your foundation, it's time to start putting things on it. Having a controlled Internet presence is only the first step. It gives you ways to promote your work, but that means that the next step is to have work to promote in the first place. There are many ways to do this, depending on your current skills and situation.

In some cases, you can put a bit of polish on a product from your existing work. Sometimes you can reference freelance or open source project work you've done. This is where things start to get interesting.

Some organizations are very open and take the attitude that what you do on your own time is your own business. Most are relatively open so long as what you do does not create a conflict of interest with your primary line of work. Some of the larger ones are more restrictive and will threaten you with legal action if you do not get permission ahead of time.

In all of these cases, though, there are ways to shift into the public sphere.

Becoming Public

Remember that no company will hire you unless you stand a good chance of making more money for it than you cost. Remember also that daily progress towards your goal comes first. The people that you want to be hired by also follow this rule. If you can't help them make daily progress to their goal, they're not going to give you an offer.

The more private you are, as a person and with your work, the harder it will be to demonstrate to an organization that you can help it out. However, the more you do publicly, the better others can verify your claims. Admittedly, moving from a private world to a public one can be extremely difficult. You may not be able to do this from where you are, but over the course of a career, you could move in that direction. There are two things to keep in mind.

First, always make sure your work benefits someone else. This is a more concise way of saying that no one is going to give you a job unless they get more out of it than you do. There is nothing wrong with that; after all, that is how an economy works. Many people climb the corporate ladder to get into a higher place on the hierarchy, achieving greater status and more money along the way. However, the people who wind up in a position to hire others often have clear goals. It is easier to achieve goals with more than one person, so the people hiring you need your help. Basically, without you, they cannot accomplish their own goals. That, right there, is your leverage.

Second, where possible, be seen helping others. The more public your work is, the easier it is to demonstrate what you can do. So the trick here is to join these two ideas. If you want to make your work more public and your company wants to use you to advance its goals, make one dependent on the other.

Open Source Projects
One of the easiest ways to be public in what you do is to join an open source project. Most people view these projects from a programming perspective; however, there are other options. Open source projects exist because their creators want to meet a need (or, frankly, just to play with new technology, but it should be obvious to tell when you're looking at a hobby project). This means that successful projects often increase in complexity at a rate that technology alone can't maintain. As projects get more complex, they begin to need more people in non-technical roles. These may be project managers, technical support people, or technical writers. Since many people avoid these roles, these are often easy ways to join a project and rapidly build a work portfolio that you can show off. As impressive as technical work on an open

source project can be, this type of nontechnical work can be even more impressive to employers, as it shows the ability to work with projects at a higher level.

This is all well and good if you work somewhere that encourages you to experiment with open source technologies or doesn't care what you do in your evenings. If you work somewhere that is less flexible, you may have to find an open source project that makes it easier for you to accomplish specific goals for the organization. This way, you can demonstrate a better solution, lower cost, or faster execution—all things that your boss may be swayed by. Getting permission to use the technology could be a challenge in some arenas, but if you can demonstrate that it works (ideally, if you did the work on your own time), you can often get permission to use it. This creates a platform on which you can build, doing a small project here and there to help your organization more efficiently reach its goals.

Freelance

Freelance work is great, though hard to get at times. The common joke/complaint is that you need experience to get experience. Freelance work is much like open source work, except that you get money out of the deal. Unlike open source work, though, freelancing is generally harder to clear with your primary employer.

You have two choices. You can clear it with your boss, or you can just do it, and try not to get caught. While your ethics are your own business, be aware that getting caught could not only end your job, it could end your career. For most, the risk isn't worth it, so you'll want to get permission. If you want to persuade your current employer to let you become more public in your work, the first step is to ensure that the freelance work you're going to do does not conflict with your primary work. Clearly, you shouldn't do work for one of your competitors; however, you shouldn't put yourself into any other conflicts of interest. Such conflicts could include working for firms that compete against your current employer or doing work that would compete on its own. Thus, if your primary job is internal system administration, it's probably okay to help friends manage their servers. However, if your primary job is helping a variety of small businesses manage their servers, it would be a conflict of interest to engage in this work outside of your firm. You also should avoid doing any outside work that could "productize" what you do for your employer, as this would cause a similar conflict by using your primary line of work to generate a potentially competing income stream. Anything else is fair game so long as your boss knows about it and you have permission in writing. This means that a great many options are on the table:

- Developing noncompeting software
- Writing manuals or other documentation
- Creating build systems/infrastructure
- Writing or editing books or articles
- Managing systems for organizations
- Volunteering your various skills at nonprofit organizations

The list can go on and on.

Once you know what you want to do, come up with a way for the freelance work to advance your value to your primary organization. This can often be couched in terms of training or R&D. Identify what you expect to learn from the freelance engagement, map out what it would cost your company to get you trained in that area, and position it as a free learning opportunity. Once you have an initial agreement, usually on something small, you can expand the scope through notification. A typical progression is as follows:

- January – Get approved to do an edit of a technical book on a subject that has some relevance to your current or potential future work. Identify a training class costing $1,500 that covers the same material as the book. Write a letter listing the cost of the class and any travel, lodging, and meals costs that it would incur. Identify the cost to the business for the time out of the office. Then compare this to the amount (zero) that it would cost the company to let you do this on your own time. Also work up an approval document stating that the company you currently work for authorizes you to do this work. Have a meeting with your boss and lay out the proposition that you be allowed to do this work, and that the other company will be tossing you some money to make up for the weekends you'll be losing to the work. Make sure your company understands that there is no conflict of interest here and that your daily work will not suffer. It should be fairly easy to get permission. If you get turned down, try to determine why and if there's a way to negotiate an option that gets you what you want. This will be good practice for the eventual negotiation for the new job. If the company doesn't want you getting paid for work, see if they'll let you freelance for free. After all, the point is to gain experience. If they don't want you doing the work at all, see if they'll allow you a smaller project, then grow it from there.

- April – Get approved to do another edit of a technical book. Email your boss saying something like "I got another tech editing opportunity. Can you just email me back saying it's okay?" Then document that return email, along with the signed approval document from January.

- August – Land a writing assignment for a magazine. This blurs the lines between editing and writing, but that's okay because you're trying to grow your portfolio, so anything counts. Email your boss again and ask for permission. Store this permission as well.

- October – Get another freelance gig. Email your boss with something like "I don't want to keep bugging you with these. I'm going to just maintain a list of everything I'm doing so you can check to verify that there's no conflict of interest here. If you want me to do something different, let me know."

And generally, from there on out, you have free rein to do any non-conflicting freelance work you want. As these gigs grow, you can document them on your résumé, and if they are public, you can build a list of work you've done that can be externally verified. Most editing and writing work will have your name in the work somewhere. Works for hire won't, but you can often negotiate a letter from your freelance employer that verifies that you did the work for them. This can be a great way to build your portfolio over time.

Repurposing Work Products

The last, and riskiest, method of content creation is to repurpose what you do for your day job for personal branding. If done correctly, this can be a great way to accelerate portfolio creation. However, if done poorly, it can get you fired and, potentially, sued ... so tread carefully.

If you currently have a job and are planning to play 'the long game' to change positions, this approach will be useful. If you're currently out of work, you can't easily get permission from your previous employers to reuse work you've done for them. Thus, the risk of doing so will likely be too high for you to try anything here. You may want to just skip ahead to the Brand Management section.

Fundamentally, the issue turns on how your current employer views the work you do for them. There are myriad employment handbooks and contracts out there that make it abundantly clear that the work you do for the company is not yours. This is, of course, their prerogative. After all, they're not hiring you because you're nice but for how they can use you to advance their own goals.

However, much as you can work a process to get freelancing jobs, you can also work a process to become more public with the internal work you do. While it is unlikely that you will be allowed to release your organization's intellectual property, you can slowly become more involved with intellectual products that are used outside the company. The ultimate goal here is to work on things that drive revenue by helping to get more customers or clients but that one does not need to be a client or customer to get.

Focusing on tasks that drive revenue makes it much easier to justify your value to the organization and, by extension, to any other company for which you want to work. This shift brings with it stress, as what you're doing is more noticeable by others. You'll want to embrace this stress, as this attention is what you are striving for.

The magic comes when you can shift your focus from serving the public at a profit to your organization to serving the public for free. This may seem like a conflict, but it's truly a process. The way it works is that you first get permission from your current organization to do more public work, as it directly helps the financial position of your firm. Then, you take some of that work and try to get the company to simply release it, as you've already been paid for it and free items boost the brand position of the firm itself.

As an example, suppose you are in charge of network monitoring. Currently, your company uses you to keep an eye on how the network is working, but you realize that you can use your tools to do more. By opening up access to one of your tools, you can prove to your customers that your services are running. By adding to the list of what's being monitored, you can help your customers by monitoring their systems for them. As time goes by, you can open up more and more of the system to your company's customers and provide different services to them: demonstrate uptime and downtime metrics to simplify trouble-shooting, limit service disruption to help your company win renewals, or show premium customers that they have priority.

It doesn't matter why you make such a change, it just matters that you do. This moves your activity from "internal" (i.e., company over-head) to "revenue generating" or, at the very least, "revenue defend-ing." Collect metrics for how much money your work has made (or saved) the company. This gets you halfway there. The next step requires a bit of marketing or sales work but may be worth the effort.

Once you've done the work to justify your own existence, defend your work from the customer's perspective. Think of how the work you've done benefits them. Document this benefit, first free-form, with no length limits and with no particular focus on the rules of grammar. Then, go through and make it more generic. Remove anything that could identify your customer. Replace business names. Working at companies like Target or Walmart can become "worked for a large international retailer"; interning for Fat Tony can become "interned at a local financial services institution." Replace people's names with their roles, such as "CEO" or "Assistant to the Vice President of Laundry Services."

Once this is done, start trimming. Aim to get down to three para-graphs. Replace overly labyrinthine articulations with simple words. If you are certain you can't cut anymore and it's still too long, let it sit for a day, then try again in the morning. If that fails, enlist the help of a friend. Most writing can be cut a lot further than you think.

Finally, go through the three paragraphs and highlight or bold the words and phrases that other customers similar to your current custo-mers would find most useful. Phrases like "reduced turnover by 80%" and "increased sales by 150%" are good. Use this information to create a one-page marketing document, using clip art or public photography. Work your organization's colors (using a color tool to pick the hex codes off your firm's website) into headers, primary fonts, etc. You can often get the name of the font from your company's website by going to "View Source" and seeing what they're using. (More on this topic later.)

Take the marketing document to your friends and get their feedback. Tweak it repeatedly until it looks right, then present it to your boss or someone in sales. See if they can use it to bring in new business. As soon as someone sends it out, it becomes public, and thus fair game for you to put in your portfolio. The more of these you do, the easier it will become, and the bigger your portfolio can get. A bigger portfolio means more stories. The more stories you have, the easier it will be to talk to interviewers about how awesome you are.

Sensitive Environments

If you work in a sensitive environment, such as a governmental, military, or research and development firm, you may not be able to repurpose any work safely. A good rule of thumb is that if you signed a nondisclosure agreement (NDA) with your organization or your organization's customers, don't even try to reuse that work. If you work in a job with a clearance and you don't know with absolute certainty that the items you're considering using have been declassified, don't use them.

Getting a job that fits you perfectly is worth some risk. It is not, however, worth risking going to jail over. Be smart here.

PERSONAL BRAND MANAGEMENT

It's not enough to just create your brand; you have to manage it as well. To a large extent, it will be self-managing, but there are two things you should keep in mind for the long run: networking and search engine optimization (SEO).

Networking

If you are like the majority of technical employees out there, you suck at talking about yourself. That will be addressed in a bit. Despite that, you must get out there and network with others. If you don't, the first time you really have to talk about yourself will be in an interview. First tries never work well.

At least once a week, don't go home after work. Find a group to join. Odds are there is a technically focused user group in your field somewhere nearby. User groups come in all flavors: Linux, Agile, .NET, Java, Oracle, Cisco, COBOL, data management, IT auditing, etc. Spend some time on the search engines and find one. Go onto

Meetup.com and see what peripherally interesting groups exist that you could join. Then, join up and start introducing yourself to people. If there is a topic you feel comfortable presenting, and that doesn't create conflicts with your current employer, consider offering to present at a meeting. Once you land your job, keep attending. At that point it'll be your turn to give back. People in those groups can tell when folks are there to connect with the community and when they're just using the community for help. People don't tend to look very highly on people who abuse social groups this way and will be much less likely to help you the next time around.

If you're particularly brave and/or willing to take risks, consider joining a leads group such as BNI or a speaking group like Toastmasters. These groups are aimed more at sales types, to generate sales leads for one another, but they can be very powerful for technical folk. Remember, every new job you pursue will have an element of competition to it. If your competition is all introverted people focused on technology, it just takes a little bit of business acumen to set you apart.

Of course, you're not going to join a group like this and suddenly be able to make a ton of sales, nor will you become a presentation master overnight. You will, however, gradually become better than average—and that's all you need to get noticed. Simply being able to speak about your area of expertise to those outside your background is enormously powerful and well worth spending a year to learn how to do. There are additional presentation resources in the Resources appendix at the end of the book.

SEO Cycles

Search engine optimization (SEO) is like thermodynamics. You can't win, you can't break even; and you can't not play. That said, you do not need to be an expert. People who focus on SEO will give you tips for beating the search engines. However, this turns into an arms race between the people running the search engines, who want to split priority between the quality of returned results and those who pay them to run ads ... and the SEO tycoons who want the exact opposite.

You can't not play the SEO game; however, you should play as little as possible.

Analyze the platform you selected for your website and/or blog. Look at its SEO plugins and load the one that seems the most popular. Spend an evening learning how to use it, then set it up. Connect your site to Google Webmaster tools and start working through the issues raised. Then, stop. Shift your focus from optimization to content creation. It doesn't matter how well-ranked you are if you're not saying anything. Just stay focused on content creation and revisit your SEO every three months or so. Any more than that and you're allowing yourself to be distracted from your goal.

CHAPTER 2

Time to Leave: How to Know When You Should Move On

THE END OF THE ROAD

When you're driving somewhere, and the road you're on is about to end, there are usually clear warning signs. Sometimes the signs are literal and say things like "Dead End" or "Bridge Is Out." Other times, they're more subtle; you start to notice that the road isn't being maintained very well, there are fewer people on it, and it doesn't seem to continue past that cliff up ahead. In either case, it's generally considered a good idea to move onto another road before, not after, the one you're on comes to an end.

In business, doing this can be tricky. Many people don't actively manage their careers and only think about job hunting when they are unemployed. This is stressful and demoralizing, so this chapter focuses on identifying when to start looking. People have said for generations that it's easier to find a job if you have a job. This is only partly true. It takes a lot of time out of your life to be job hunting while working your current job, but if you can manage to string jobs together without large gaps, it makes life a lot easier—both financially and emotionally.

ECONOMIC CYCLES

Traditional businesses exist to make money. Traditional nonprofits exist to advance a cause. Traditional government jobs exist, in theory, to help other people. When the economy is growing, all of these organizations do well. However, when the economy falters, it becomes harder for organizations to achieve these goals.

This book does not have space to dig into macro- and microeconomic theory, or even the specifics of how market economics work within an industry, so some corners have to be cut. Instead of an economic treatise, here's an analogy—think about money as water. This is how business owners think, and the more attention you can pay to the business, the better position you'll be in.

Imagine there's a stream of water running as far as the eye can see. Various people use this stream, carrying buckets daily to get the water they need. There are also mills running large waterwheels to grind grain for flour, spin fiber into thread, and the like. So long as the water flows, everyone is fine. However, as the water level begins to drop, whether due to a general drought or because people are consuming more water than is feeding the stream, the system begins to fail.

First, people who had some water saved up at home have advantages over those who did not. Then, the mills with smaller waterwheels start to shut down, as their wheels just don't go deep enough. Then, eventually, the larger mills fail as well.

The economic problem here is that of uncertainty. Some droughts last only a season, some last for many years, and some are permanent. All the mill owners must decide for themselves which situation they're in and take appropriate action. Each individual person must do the same. Some people will go to another stream, but if a majority of people do that, those who stay behind will have a significant advantage, with the whole stream to themselves. Conversely, if no one leaves, the stream will dry up all the faster.

That's what it's like in an industry when a recession hits, or when a new technology comes through that makes the industry less valuable. By paying attention to how your organization works and how the money flows through it, you're effectively monitoring the economic health (stream level) of your industry. If your former steady stream of new clients or work for existing clients has shifted to only occasional work, that's an indicator that a drought may be coming. This can be hard to detect, and many businesses facing this problem will start going after bigger and bigger clients in the hope that one big project will save the company. Sometimes it can, but it is a very risky approach, and if it doesn't pan out, layoffs will often be on the near horizon.

Keep track of how your competitors are doing. Odds are that you know someone outside of your company but still in your industry. Check in with them once in a while to see how busy they are. If your competition is doing well and your organization is not, it may be a management/sales issue and not one of overall economics.

At a personal level, keep an eye on the hiring ads for your skills. Some job sites allow you to save job searches and will even provide results to you by email or RSS on an ongoing basis. Keeping an eye on these can be a great measure as to whether the economic issues are focused on your geographic area, your industry, or are global. For example, a search on the CISSP and GCIH certifications showed the following patterns: In 2006, there was an average of about 10 hits per week for those certifications in the upper Midwest. During the recession of 2008, the average dropped to between zero and one. At the time this book is being written, it is up well over 30 per week.

During a global economic downturn, it will be hard to find a company willing to take a risk on hiring you. If your current company is stable and otherwise tolerable (no abusive bosses, no pressure to engage in illegal or unethical activity), you may just want to ride it out. If, however, the economic issues are localized, consider moving. The last several recessions in the US were felt last and recovered from first within the Midwest. Cities further from the coast, such as Chicago, Illinois, Omaha, Nebraska, and Minneapolis, Minnesota, were sheltered from the massive ups and downs that were experienced by cities like San Francisco and New York. Of course, moving to a better job climate during a poor localized economy is not always an option. There are issues of social connections, financial costs involved in moving, and emotional costs in leaving where you are and forming new connections where you're going. However, if these do not seem burdensome to you, consider looking further afield for a place to work. It doesn't have to be a permanent move; moving somewhere else for a few years just to gain experience can do wonders for your overall career.

Finally, if the downturn is industry-specific, consider changing industries. This is where your saved job searches can be incredibly useful. If jobs in your industry have dropped to near zero but jobs availability in other industries where you possess skills have not changed in frequency, it may be time to shift your focus. Some industries permanently contract because of powerful factors such as automation, consumerization, or fashion. There are, for example, a lot fewer people needed to help build cars because robots are cheap now. Similarly, fancy women's hats are a lot less popular than they were in the early 1900s, so there are a lot fewer milliners.

If you see problems, learn enough about your region and your industry to take a reasonable guess as to the cause. This will help you protect yourself. Your bosses will be focusing on their own jobs. The owners/boards of the organization will be focusing on achieving their goals. You need to look out for yourself.

Maturity

Organizations, like people, grow and change over time. Simplified, this growth follows a pattern, beginning as a start-up or a small business that attracts more and more customers (or investors) and goes through several changes. It's not uncommon for an organization to start as a "cowboy" style business, where everyone is trusted to do their own thing. Then, as the organization grows, it shifts to a system that is guided a bit more by management than by trust. This works for a while, but direct management often stops working well, and the organization focuses more on communication and documentation. This typically continues as other firms are acquired and the policy and procedures begin to merge. In the end, you often see extremely large multinational companies with numerous layers of management. This pattern can be seen in Figure 2.1, below.

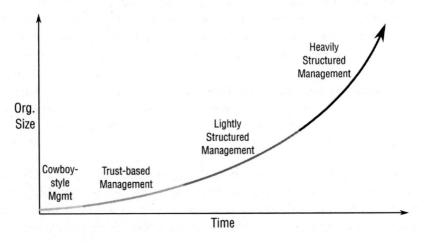

Figure 2.1 Organizational Maturity

This pattern has additional effects. In smaller organizations, because there are fewer layers of management and fewer policies restricting employees, individual employees often have more flexibility in how they work. At this scale, it is common to hear things like "so long as the work gets done, I don't care." At larger scales, organizations tend to lose this flexibility but gain in stability. It's easier to "coast" in these organizations but harder to do creative work.

There's nothing wrong with any particular mode of working, but you may find that, as your organization changes around you, you become less comfortable. There are many types of culture change. One very common one is when your organization gets acquired. Changes can be from a procedural and documented way of working to one that follows Lean or Agile principles. This can involve a loss of flexibility or a contraction of your role. Basically, as things change, you can find yourself longing for things to be the way they used to be and growing less and less comfortable where you are.

If you feel like the corporate culture has shifted and is now at odds with who you fundamentally are, it's time to leave. However, figuring out why things changed on you, and what you really need, can be helpful in determining what job area to target.

IDENTIFYING WHAT YOU WANT

If your environment feels "off," and you can't trace it to specific issues involving the economy or corporate growth, try to determine what's going on. Think about the last time you were happy at work. What were you working on? With whom were you working? Did the project have a level of personal meaning that is lacking now? Was there a style of work that is no longer available to you? Did your team grow or shrink to a point where you were no longer comfortable?

This topic can (and has) make many a book in and of itself. The important thing here is to focus specifically on what you need to thrive in a new job. The rest of this process involves a *lot* of after-hours work, and culminates in creating a job that fits your needs precisely. However, if you don't know where you want to go, you're never going to get there. By focusing not on "What can I do?" or even "What do I want to do?" but instead on "What I can do that gives me back at least as much energy as I put in?", you will develop a self-sustaining career whose pursuit feels more like a game than drudgery.

This is a very personal decision and one that must be made more by feel than anything else.

●●●

The Story of Josh

My first job out of college was at a small company with about eight employees. I was very much in the "I need a job, any job" mode when I got it, and happened to luck into a job that gave me carte blanche in how I worked, even if it didn't pay as well as those of my peers. I got to figure out *how* to work at the same time I was figuring out how to develop software and hardware appliances. It was a great fit until the company was sold; it suddenly grew from 14 employees (by then) to well over 100. At the same time, the culture became much more restrictive and shifted from a start-up professional atmosphere to an established blue-collar 9 to 5 culture where the developers were treated the same as the factory workers. I didn't know what was wrong at the time, but knew I had to move on, and I found a company that was smaller and more flexible.

The new job lasted for many years, but the company was, again, acquired. After the acquisition, things got a bit more restrictive, but it wasn't all that bad. Instead, the new company just had a slower way of working than was my preference. After sticking that out for a while, I realized that I had goals for the sort of work I wanted to do. My work had to have meaning and pay me reasonably well, but most importantly, I wanted the flexibility to try new things and move as quickly as I wanted when implementing new ideas. That realization inspired my long-term—over two years—effort to find a company willing to let me work how and where I wanted to work, doing what I wanted to do in a way that advanced everyone's goals.

As I found potential employers and interviewed at them, I kept focused on the question of whether this company would do a better job of helping me achieve my goals than where I already was. In many cases, the answer was "no," so I stayed put. Eventually, I found one where the answer was "yes"; my focus on what I wanted and how to get it enabled me to get the job I wanted.

This process is not a fast one, but once you finally figure out where you want to be, the success rate can be extremely high. This is a worthwhile approach, as the alternative is years of hating your job and feeling trapped.

CHAPTER 3

Résumés and Cover Letters: Why the Common Approach Only Works against You

RÉSUMÉS CLOSE DOORS

The traditional approach of creating a résumé and blasting it to all available job openings is one that is doomed to failure. Why? Think about it from the perspective of hiring managers. Even in a relatively small city, over one hundred résumés can quickly inundate them as the résumés keep coming and coming. In large cities, a job posting could garner well over a thousand responses.

No one is actually going to read that many résumés.

So what happens instead? If there is no hiring software in use, someone is going to sit down with the stack and do a rapid sort. Most managers will first filter out everyone who lacks a college degree. This is, of course, not fair. However, it *is* a filter that can cut out half of the applicants. In technical fields, if the stack is still too large, they often filter out people who lack certifications. Then, they often look for years of experience and pick those with a lot of experience but with job titles that indicate lower salaries. Only at that point, with a stack of five to ten applications, are résumés actually read.

If there is hiring software in use, the process is only slightly different. First, the job is assigned a series of keywords and any résumé that doesn't match a certain percentage of those keywords is filtered out. Those that pass go through the same process as above.

So in the end, that beautiful résumé you sweated over and made perfect is more likely to get you excluded from a job than considered for it. If you don't play the keyword guessing game the way the hiring manager wants you to, you're out. If you don't fit the pattern (experience, degrees, certifications), you're out. The résumé is there to make it easier for companies to exclude people. What you want is the exact opposite. You need a tool that makes it more likely for you to succeed.

NETWORKING OPENS DOORS

The easiest way to get something, anything, is to ask for it. Fundamentally, people like to help other people. The psychology around this involves reciprocity and altruism. Basically, people will help you because, at some point, they may need help themselves or just because it feels good to do so. While few people are in a position to hire you just because you ask, it's amazing how helpful it can be to just go up to someone, introduce yourself, tell them how much you want to work for their organization, and ask for their help. Sometimes you may need to bribe them with a drink or meal to get them to open up to you, but simply asking is the most powerful tool you have.

If you are looking in a geographic area you've lived in for a while, or have a reasonably large Internet-based social network, you should have a list of people willing to help you. Dedicated "networking events" are unlikely to help you here. You're going to get the most help from picking your target organization, finding out who works there or who has worked there, and seeing how they relate to the people you know. Sites like LinkedIn and Plaxo have made this a whole lot easier than it used to be, so spend some time exploring. Keep in mind what you are looking for so you can avoid wasting too much time on the Internet. If someone is not in a position to hire you, look first for their connections. If there are no connections you can use, move on. If there are, then it's worth digging a bit deeper to figure out how to convince them to give you an introduction, should you need one. In general, you should not be spending more than three minutes on any particular person at this stage.

Once you know who to talk to, you can start working on your pitch. This is covered in greater detail in later chapters.

COVER LETTERS OPEN DOORS

If you can't find a personal connection to a potential interviewer in your target company, even by tracing to friends of friends of friends, you'll need to introduce yourself with a "letter." The word letter is in quotes because the term "cover letter" no longer means what it once did. It used to refer to a letter of introduction that you would send with your résumé or portfolio. It would introduce yourself, explain why you want to work there, what you'd bring to the organization, and request a meeting. These days, however, there are often more cover letters than can be read, so they're filtered, too.

Instead, people are starting to switch to other ways of attracting attention. Your "letter" could be an introduction video on the web. It could be a custom website such as Matthew Epstein did with google-pleasehire.me. It could be an infographic such as those created by Keith Bates (www.kbates.com) or generated by vizualize.me. There are many options. However, in all cases, the letter should do three things.

Catch Attention

A letter, whatever its form, is useless unless it is read. You must make it interesting enough that, in half a second, the person seeing it decides that it's worth his or her time to dig deeper. There are many ways to do this. In a letter, you could open with a claim that seems overly strong or counterfactual. Marketers do this all the time; while it feels a bit sleazy, it does work. So long as you explain in the piece why you're not lying, it's perfectly fine. You can also make the letter exceptionally short, craft it like a full-page magazine ad, or resort to gimmicks.

If you're doing an infographic, make sure it uses good design principles and attracts the eye. Consider getting help from an artist if this is not your skill set.

If you're doing a video, look at how trailers work. People watch movies for a reason. Look at how the trailers suck you in and make you want to see the whole video.

Explain the Benefits of Hiring You

No one cares why you want to work there. They're not going to hire you because you're good at flattery. They're going to hire you because, by doing so, they can achieve their goals with either higher levels of certainty or lower cost. That's it. Try to explain how hiring you would help along those two dimensions. If you can make the business case that hiring you is a good idea, you can go to the next part of the "letter." If you can't make a good business case, you're not ready and shouldn't waste anyone's time.

Ask for a Meeting

Finally, you need to ask them to meet with you. This could be a phone call, an email, or, ideally, a face-to-face meeting. The entire effort is wasted if you don't get a meeting, and unless you actually ask for a meeting, you're unlikely to get one.

Basically, you've crafted the beginning of the piece so the viewer spends half a second deciding to invest five to ten minutes in you. The entire piece then exists to convince the viewer to invest one to two hours in you. For a lot of business people, one to two hours is quite an investment, but by this time, you've already convinced them—twice—that you're worth some effort. Then, all you have to do is get them to invest a bit more in you each time you meet. Eventually, so much effort will be sunk into you that the only way they can learn more about you is to give you a job. The structure of the interest-building letter can be seen in Figure 3.1, below.

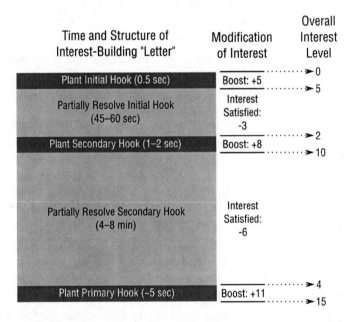

Figure 3.1 Growth of Interest: Showing Amount of Time Spent by Target Reading Letter and Resulting Change in Target's Interest Level in you as a Candidate.

USING RÉSUMÉS TO TELL STORIES

Résumés are not inherently worthless. As a "getting attention" tool, a résumé is useful for getting search engines to notice you. A well-written résumé will garner annoying calls and emails from recruiters all over the world. These calls are aimed at getting you to do work you've done before for people who want to pay a recruiting firm substantially more than they are willing to pay you. These tend to be short-run jobs, but you can string such jobs together into a career. Sadly, this career collapses completely once the world decides your skills are no longer worth what recruiters charge. When this happens, the market quickly contracts, rendering that set of skills worthless.

Approaching work from a pure skill-for-hire basis like this makes it difficult to develop new skills, so while it can be lucrative for a while, it seldom lasts long enough to constitute a career ... so this book focuses on another method.

A Note on Recruiters

Being a recruiter can be extremely lucrative. The business model is such that recruiters collect a portion of the salary of every person they place, for a certain amount of time. However, their business model also requires that they sustain this model to keep the money flowing. In most cases, if you are placed by a recruiter at a firm in a permanent role, he or she only collects a portion of your salary for a year or two. Thus, recruiters have strong incentives to keep a new flow of people moving through their system. This is easily done by placing people in roles that are poor fits so they eventually move on, thus giving the recruiter both vacancies and unemployed people to exploit.

For individual recruiters, it's a numbers game. The more people they place, the more money they make. The goal is to spend the least amount of time necessary to place any individual. Thus, recruiters tend to work off of résumés by matching basic credentials and running people through the system as quickly as possible. This approach is completely opposite of the slow, long-term approach described in this book.

If all you need is a job, any job, try a recruiter. Maybe you'll find a good one, but you should plan on having to restart the process again relatively soon.

If you want a long-term career that allows you to grow and think, you will need more flexibility than most recruiters allow. Since the economic models are in opposition, it's best to avoid recruiters as much as you can. The one exception here is if you can manage to work the system to your advantage. This would involve structuring a deal where you convince the recruiter that working with you will be considerably more lucrative than the average engagement. This might convince them to actually work on getting you introduced to the sorts of companies you want to work for.

If you must work with a recruiter, apply the entire process in this book to the recruiters themselves. There are a surprising number of unethical people in the world and, sadly, this particular industry attracts many of them. While there is no way to guarantee that you will be completely protected, you can do better than average by fully vetting the people with whom you work, whether it be a future employer or just the person who helps you get there.

The other way to use a résumé is to structure it for rapid story reference. People respond extremely well to stories. A well-structured story builds rapport between the storyteller and listener. It is more memorable than a straightforward retelling of facts. Since the advent of radio and television, we have developed a culture full of people who are primed to hear stories but remarkably bad at telling them. This means that you can gain a significant edge over other people just by spending a bit of time prepping your stories before you tell them.

There are many places that will teach you how to tell a good story. You can find them yourself or refer to a few good ones in the Resources section. To keep things simple here, remember that good stories have characters with which the listener can empathize, a challenge that needs to be met (or a lesson that must be learned), and a successful conclusion. There are, of course, other types of stories, but you want stories that get you hired.

Take some time and consider the challenges you've experienced in your career. Think about how you met them and what you learned from the process. Think about who was involved and to which people your prospective interviewer(s) might be sympathetic. Then, on an index card, write out each story as a series of bullet points.

- Introduce the problem
- Why was problem the significant?
- Who was affected by the problem?
- Who was the person to whom the interviewer may be sympathetic? (Person X)
- What challenges prevented any solution that might seem obvious?
- What did you try that didn't work? Why?
- What did you finally do that solved the problem for Person X?

If applicable, see if you can flavor the story with information regarding the project's budget and timeline, the number of people working with you on it, and how the ultimate success or failure affected the business.

Now, flip the index card over and, in one line, summarize the solution in a way that explains what you did and, if possible, what benefit it gave to your organization.

This process will take a while. If you're done in an afternoon, you probably didn't spend enough time. It is critical to devote enough attention to the process to make it work for you. These stories will form the basis of not only this job search, but every other job search you will do from this point on. When you're done, you should have a nice stack of index cards that, if you were to type out all the summaries, would fill a standard piece of paper—because that's what you're going to do next.

CREATING AND TUNING A MASTER RÉSUMÉ

As mentioned before, your résumé is about stories. A well-crafted résumé will consist of a list of stories that, if told in series, would give the interviewer both a good understanding of what you did in each role and also show how what you've done can directly help the interviewer with his or her needs. Of course, any job will have more stories than will be of interest to your interviewer. So the way to target the résumé is to start with significantly more stories than you need, then weed out the less interesting stories for each job to which you want to apply.

Take your stack of index cards and group them by job/role, sort the jobs by time with the most recent first, and start typing them up with one bulleted list per job stack. If you have between two and five years of experience, this should take a page or two. If you have five to ten years' worth, it should take two to three. If you have over ten, it should go well over three. That stuff about a one-page résumé is garbage. That's to make it easier for people to filter you out. You want to be filtered *in,* so you need material to work with.

After you make this list of lists, add a one-line header to each bulleted list that provides the job title, the company name, and the start and stop dates. Prospective employers care about gaps, not dates, so month and year are sufficient here.

At the top of your résumé, add a short Profile section. In no more than the top fifth of the page put your name, any certifications you have, and your email address and phone number. If you're feeling witty, add a byline that describes you in a single line. Avoid business speak: "Ambitious Over-Achiever Focused On Driving Business Value For Customers And Shareholders" tells a pretty boring story. "Creative Thinker, Developer, and Sculptor" tells a much more interesting one.

Now, to whip the rest of the document into shape. Choose a reasonable font and type size for your lists. It should be no smaller than 11-point. The font is up to you, but keep it professional. If you need help, check out Julian Hansen's awesome font choice infographic (julianhansen.com/files/infographiclarge_v2.png) or just use Georgia, which is designed for readability on monitors and is present on all Windows PCs. Once that's done, tighten up each story summary that extends past a single line so everything fits at one bullet per line and looks pretty. This makes them easier to read and can dramatically reduce the amount of space your résumé takes up. A self-consistent résumé is much more powerful than one that isn't, and keeping the résumé down to one line per story makes it much easier to scan.

There will be some stories that will look as if they cannot be shortened. This is wrong. If you get stuck, set the résumé aside for a couple of days and revisit those lines. If you still can't do it, get someone to help you. Maybe your story is really two stories. Maybe you've been overly wordy and need to cut. Or maybe that story doesn't belong in the résumé at all. If you can't fit a story in a single line, you probably can't tell it to your interviewer in a way he or she can understand it. Edit yourself mercilessly.

In an actual interview, you need to be able to review the résumé quickly, be reminded of your story card, and tell the story. By keeping each story reminder short enough to read quickly, you improve your interview flow and gain the ability to jump straight into the bit that matters—storytelling.

The story you tell must be focused on your target. There are almost certainly stories that you do not want to tell to your targeted interviewer, as they may be irrelevant or convey an impression that you don't want. Since your résumé is now a list of bullet points, simply make a copy of the file and remove all the bullets that you don't want to talk about. This is where you get it down to a single page—but instead of a generic single page that tries to cover everything, this is a page of pure gold, full of stories you can tell that make you sound awesome. The interview will then consist of the interviewer pointing to something random on the page and asking you about it. You get to knock their socks off by telling a crafted story with characters and plot arc. This will be so different from any other candidate that your interview will rapidly turn into a series of stories, some of which will not be on your résumé at all, and time will fly by.

Advanced Résumé

There are many ways to structure résumés. The method described here is optimized for story flow and for people who do not have a design background. If you have more advanced graphics skills than average, consider adding color and pictures to your résumé. For inspiration, do online searches for "creative résumés." Just remember that your résumé must also be searchable, so if you do get creative with it, be sure to also make a boring version that search engines can read.

EXAMPLE RÉSUMÉ AND STORY CARDS

Examples can be helpful. While there can be no one example that directly applies to your needs, suppose you were working in an infrastructure role and wanted a new job. You've come up with some nice story cards and have targeted a résumé specifically at your interviewer. Here are some example stories and what the final targeted résumé could look like. Here, each story card has details and a summary. The summary would become a line item on the résumé, which would serve as a reminder of the entire story card.

Problem: Email issue resolution time in excess of 48 hours

Why it mattered: Upset customers threatened to leave service for competitor

Characters:
* Email Customer
* Email Administrator
* IT Manager

Attempts at resolution:
* Email tracing—failed due to routing complexities
* Anti-spam adjustments—helped a bit, but blocked too many legitimate emails

Solution:
Revised email routing process, eliminating complexity by centralizing domain processing, anti-spam, and DNS lookups, eliminating half the hops from the message route.

Summary: 90% reduction in email trouble tickets, resulting in additional resources for strategic projects.

Figure 3.2 Story Card Email

Problem: Persistent hacks on web server

Why it mattered: Web server would randomly promote Cialis and Viagra on company's website, damaging the brand.

Characters:
* Business owner
* IT Manager
* Web Administrator

Attempts at resolution:
* Removed injected code, got re-injected
* Applied updates to operating system, apache and PHP, did not stop hacks

Solution:
The attacker had gotten in due to a PHP issue, but even though the issue was fixed in the patch, the attacker had the system passwords. Changing the passwords and adjusting the firewall to require VPN access before administrative access prevented re-infection.

Summary: Detected, analyzed, and prevented recurrent intrusion into company's web server.

Figure 3.3 Story Card Web Hacks

Problem: Backups failing throughout entire server network

Why it mattered: Without solid backups, making critical system changes such as updates was extremely risky, but leaving systems unpatched also brought risks.

Characters:
* IT Manager
* Backup Administrator
* IT Team

Attempts at resolution:
* Increased storage space, failed because it took too long to backup systems
* Increased network speed between critical servers and backup server, which helped a bit, but did not provide full coverage

Solution:
Shifted backup system to use block-level and snapshotting technology so after the initial sync, full system backups could be collected several times during the day.

Summary: Implemented block-level snapshot-based backup system to reduce backup time by 80%, allowing for multiple maintenance windows throughout the week.

Figure 3.4 Story Card Failing Backups

Jennifer Quantum: Master Résumé   jenny2@authority.com
Certifications: CISSP, MCSA, MCSE: Private Cloud, PMP, VCP   555-867-5309

Profile
I am a professional with 13 years' experience in information technology. I focus on identifying and eliminating difficult problems, including external takeover, system failure, and technology misuse. Through continual improvement, I help businesses better achieve their goals.

Experience – Full Time
September 2011 – Present   *Team Leader*   *Stormwatch 2.0*

Analysis and Strategy
* Reduced email trouble ticket resolution time by 90%, supporting resource reallocation.
* Reduced backup time by 80% via block-level synchronization technologies.
* Created flow-based project methodology for internal use and guiding client projects.
* Devised rapid assessment processes for cost reduction and increased delivery speed.
* Revised annual risk assessment to focus directly on business data management needs.
* Created long-term PCI compliance strategy internal use.

Incident Management
* Detected, analyzed, and prevented recurrent intrusion into web server.
* Discovered compromised internal employee, worked with law enforcement to build case.

May 2000 – November 2008   *Incident Manager*   *Authority*

Incident Management:
* Assisted takedown of Bendix crime ring utilizing Kherubim malware.
* Project lead on the Atom and Armageddon projects, details classified.
* Worked with Carrier's engine in an analytical and preventative capacity.

Education
September 2001 – May 2005   *Arcadia*
* Bachelors Degree in Advanced Physics

Figure 3.5 Example Résumé

CHAPTER 4

Talking about Yourself: The Fine Lines around Boasting, Bragging, Belittling, and Begrudging

By now, you should have a nice set of stories about how awesome you are. This chapter is about convincing other people that you are awesome, too. There is a lot more about this process than can be covered here, so please check out the Resources section for more detail.

There are, however, two main rules.

1. Being awesome takes practice.
2. Too much practice shifts awesome into awful.

These rules are, clearly, in opposition to one another. The hardest part about telling stories is to make them sound good but unrehearsed. If you have no acting experience, it is best to err on the side of under-rehearsal, as it's hard to back it down from overdoing things. Practice by using the index cards as flash cards and telling your stories from the prompts. Do it out loud, ignoring how foolish you feel. Once you get to the point where you can tell a story, from memory, without saying "umm" or "uh," you've practiced enough. As illustrated in Figure 4.1,

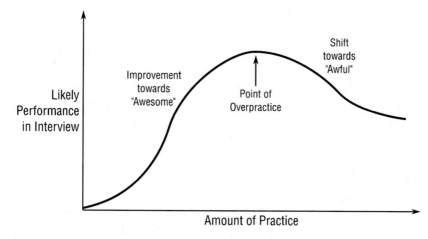

Figure 4.1 Practice Curve

you want to avoid over-practicing. You know the story and you know you can tell it. From there, it's all about how you tell it.

TELLING TIMELY STORIES

These stories will come in three types, mostly differing by time. This is where you often hear about the dreaded elevator speeches—which, theoretically, are delivered to someone prepared to listen. It's far more likely that you'll have to tell the same story three different ways: to someone who is distracted, to someone who is paying attention, and to someone who is actively involved in the story. You must be able to engage with people in any of these frames of mind, and they each require a different way to capture and hold attention.

Distracted Storytelling

When someone is distracted, you have between 30 seconds and two minutes to get your point across. Aim for the lower bound and work out a way to tell your story as quickly as possible. This should be easy, as each story is already in the form of a bulleted list. Just visualize the list, run through each point in about five seconds, and stop at the end.

Then, once you have that down, record yourself and look for areas of improvement. You don't want to be scripted, but try to eliminate as many "um"s, "uh"s, and "but"s as you can. Make sure that the story flows logically and that you didn't skip over any details that you should have explained in greater detail. Don't add details at the expense of time. The goal is to catch someone's interest, not explain absolutely everything.

Then, see if there's anything you can do to punch up the story. This will have to be on the fly, as you don't know who you'll be talking to. Just think of how you can emphasize specific portions if you're talking to a peer, someone you are mentoring, or a potential boss. Again, you don't have to be an expert. Simply putting a bit of thought into the process will raise you far above the competition.

Attentive Storytelling

When someone is paying attention, you get a bit more of their time, but still not a lot. You should be able to expand your basic story to three to five minutes. Practice with a timer so you can track the time you actually take. As you expand the story, put a bit more time into why the problem was significant. Talk about how it affected customers, employees, and the business itself. Mention any criticality; an emergency issue that you had to resolve in 30 minutes during business hours is very different from a project that you got to work on over a period of two years.

Then, talk about your problem-solving process, how you arrived at your attempted solutions (if they exist), the challenges you faced, and how you overcame them. Finally, talk about the ultimate resolution, how you determined the problem was truly fixed, and how it affected the character with whom your listener will identify.

Once you've done this a few times, you should find your sense of timing developing so you won't need the timer in an actual interview. It is very important that you only use the timer as a tool and do not grow dependent on it. Using an actual timer in an interview is a good way to completely blow it, destroying all chances to build rapport with your interviewer.

Involved Storytelling

This can also be called "interrupted" storytelling. If you have practiced short and long forms of each of your stories, there may be a tendency to become focused on completing the story, forgetting that the goal of the exercise is to make yourself seem awesome. If someone interrupts, they are trying to turn the story into a discussion. This is great. Discussions are better than stories, since they flow from topic to topic with no barriers getting in the way. If, instead, you stay focused on completing the story, once you're done, there's nothing left but another story. The process of moving from one story to another requires a prompt, which is a barrier to conversation flow.

In fact, if you tell a story and get into a discussion before the end, it creates a feeling of incompleteness for the listener. People don't like this, and will want resolution of some kind. This is why television series often use cliffhangers at the end of a season. They want the viewers to return to resolve their feeling of uncertainty. If your interviewer feels this in an interview, they'll have to invite you back for a follow-up.

To practice this, it really helps to work with friends. Explain to them that their job is to interrupt you as you tell the stories you've practiced. Get into discussions with them, and start another story at an appropriate moment. Once this stops feeling awkward, you're decently prepared.

SOCIALLY ENGINEERING YOUR AUDIENCE

This feeling of incompleteness is critical when you are trying to persuade someone that you're awesome. People like to wrap things up and file them away once they're understood. If you fully explain everything, there's no reason to have another discussion. A storyteller's job is simply to keep the audience interested in the tale, possibly with pauses for momentary contributions from the audience at cliffhangers. Once the story is over, the listeners move on. But you're telling stories as a means to an end; getting the story completely told is not your primary goal.

If you identify what interests listeners and plant "hooks" in one story to get them to ask a leading question about another, you can build on this interest—over time, they wind up more interested in you than they were when they started. In addition to this making the story you're telling more interesting and flow from point to point, this is a key to getting a second interview or having a discussion about actually being hired.

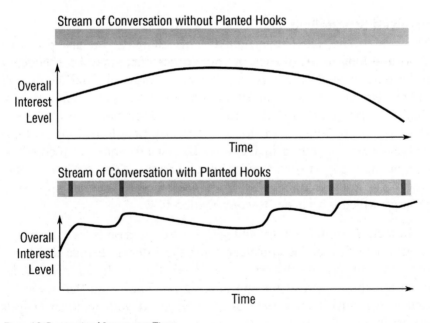

Figure 4.2 Conversational Interest over Time

For example, you might be interviewed by someone interested in science fiction and active in charities. If you identify this ahead of time (see the chapters on Reconnaissance and Metaphor Mapping), you can spin your stories using *Star Wars* metaphors and referencing the plights of those less fortunate. This sets the stage for building rapport and increases the chance of having the opportunity to launch into another story.

Clearly, you don't want to do this with every story or it will become obvious what you're doing; but if you just sprinkle these hooks into your stories here and there, you get to resolve fewer stories and lay the groundwork for a very interesting discussion.

WHAT TO AVOID

It's hard to tell good stories about yourself without coming off as a braggart. This is excellently explained in Peggy Klaus's book *Brag!: The Art of Tooting Your Own Horn without Blowing It*. In a nutshell, though, remember that everything you say and do is about other people. When you make it all about you, they tend to close down and stop listening. Any story about something awesome you did should really be about how the awesome thing you did helped someone else. The four Bs to avoid involve forgetting this rule of thumb.

Boasting and Bragging involve self-obsession. If you fall into this trap, you are saying things like: "I built a three-tier virtualization environment all by myself!" or "It took a lot of late nights, but I led my team to victory!" These are "I" statements, which aren't always bad; but if you find yourself using "I" statements with explanation points and not discussing how you helped others, you are likely boasting or bragging.

Belittling and Begrudging involve putting others down. If you do this, you'll find yourself speaking negatively about others in a way to make yourself look good. This looks like "I built a three-tier virtualization environment to help the development team. Sadly, they're too stupid to actually use it right" or "I didn't have a very good team; we had to work late nights for a month to fix some of their mistakes, but I got the team whipped into shape and we got the project done." These stories involve other people, but it makes the other people look bad and, by doing so, casts some doubt on your ability to help others.

Good versions of these stories look like: "I worked with the development team to build a three-tier virtualization system. At this time, they're using it for Development and Production, but there have been challenges adjusting their workflow to use Staging" and "There were issues in the business because the team wasn't communicating internally very well. As a group, we made mistakes, but we were able to resolve our differences over several late nights as we fixed the core problems. I'm proud to have led the team through that transition."

This approach requires a bit more humbleness and willingness to give credit to others. However, when done correctly, it makes you look all the better because you're not claiming all the credit.

PRESENTATIONS

A more formal version of storytelling is the presentation. See the Resources section for some great information on presenting. To very briefly summarize most of the advice on presenting, remember that when someone is reading, they're not listening to you. Someone who is listening to you is not reading. Someone trying to do both is going to do each badly.

So if you are presenting as part of the interview process, avoid "Death by Powerpoint" and just tell a story using the techniques in the previous section. Back this up with visual aids as appropriate, but make sure they support rather than replace what you're saying. In a nutshell, use graphics with limited words. Then, each time you change slides or show an animation, you'll recapture your audience's interest in what you're saying, but not for so long that they miss what you're saying.

CHAPTER 5

Targeting: Cyclical Filtering to Choose Targets with High Likelihoods of Success

The title of this book is *Job Reconnaissance,* but until now, it's been fairly light on what is traditionally thought of as recon. However, it's one thing to perform recon on a target and quite another to know what to do with the data you've gathered. The preceding chapters have been aimed at giving you the practice you need to properly execute on a plan to identify a target, grow their interest in you, and, eventually, get them to hire you. After all, by the time you've completed a recon engagement, it's too late to start practicing the strike. You have to be ready to go when the reconnaissance indicates it's "go" time.

This chapter digs into the actual data-gathering phase of the process, starting with target selection. Remember, as you go through this process, that the same tools and techniques that can find information about others can also be used to find information about yourself. Consider first running each task on your own name, the places you've worked, and various social media nicknames and handles. It's a good way to get some practice and it may uncover things you might want to edit or remove before you contact your target organizations.

JOB TASKS

If you've analyzed what you want to do as a job, you should have some level of understanding as to what you want your job tasks to be. You next will have figure out what sorts of industries need those tasks. This may or may not be a waste of your time. If, for example, you really just want to be a Java developer and don't much care what you develop, you only need to do some searches for companies in your target area that code in Java.

However, if you have a personal driving interest in helping people heal but your technical skills are in information architecture, you may look for health care organizations with data requirements. These could be pharmaceutical companies using "Big Data" analytics to find new drugs. They could be hospitals wanting to collect performance metrics to reduce operating room mistakes. They could be clinics aimed at lower-income people looking for ways to identify people benefiting from early outreach and increased focus on preventative care.

Basically, if you know what you want to do and can identify companies that would benefit from you doing it, add them to a list. If you can't think of any, look at the Yellow Pages (it's not much good for telephone numbers anymore) and, for each category, ask yourself, "Does this type of organization need someone like me, and if so, what would they have me do?"

JOB POTENTIAL

Some people are highly motivated not by what they do today but by what they could do tomorrow. If you are interested in long-term job growth, look for companies that support training programs. Using Google Maps to select your target and doing a "Search Nearby" search for "training" and "continuing education" can help a lot here. Search the job boards for phrases like "opportunity for growth" and "become a leader." Keep in mind that most of these are bunk, but a company that talks a good game has a higher likelihood of actually playing it than one that doesn't.

Also, keep in mind that smaller firms are more likely to let you out of the box than bigger ones. Odds are that you want a job where you are rewarded for coming up with ideas to make things better, for working hard (perhaps on your own time) to make changes, and for getting things done. When it comes to autonomy and making a difference, the smaller the business, the better.

Finally, if you want a chance to end up with lots of money at the cost of not really starting with much, consider working for a start-up. You find these by contacting investors. Search on "venture capital companies" and build a list. Then, call each one to find out if anyone they're working with needs any of your skills and mention that you are interested in creative compensation. Many such firms are starving for good talent that is willing to take the same chances the business owners are.

LOCATION AND SIZE

If you want to stay where you are, skip to the next section. If, however, you want to move somewhere else specifically, check out that area. Look for "best places to work" lists. Order the Book of Lists, as published by the business journal community for that region, from the local business-focused newspaper or journal or www.bookoflistsonline. com. Look on LinkedIn for people you may know in that area, and ask which companies you should consider.

If you want to work for a large firm there, search online footage of baseball, football, and hockey games in the area. See who advertises there. Get a map view of the city and see what their large conference centers are called. Call the local zoos and museums and see which firms donate the most money to them. The big companies like to make a splash, so you can build a list very easily. You can also get lists online, but building lists this way also tells you how involved a company is in the community; if you want to move somewhere specific, odds are that you want to be involved in the community as well.

If you want to work for a small organization, start by searching for the obvious combinations: "'IT company' 'Dallas, TX'" or "'software development' 'Seattle, WA.'" If you get stuck on type of company, go to a keyword suggester (adwords.google.com/o/KeywordTool, tools.seobook.com/keyword-tools/seobook, freekeywords.wordtracker. com, etc.) and enter the type of company you're looking for. It'll give you a nice list that you can search through one at a time, adding the city you're looking for as detailed above. For example, a search on "software development" on Google's keyword tool points out that searches on "software developers," "software developer companies," and "software application developer" would be unlikely to match the first search, so your search would grow deeper.

RATING

Most cities have "Best _____,Year__" contests, where you can learn the "Best Information Security Firm, 2012," "Best Bank, 2013," "Best Plumber, 2014," and the like. These contests are, of course, rigged. Not only do larger companies have more employees and usually garner the most votes, but they often tell their employees who to vote for in other categories. However, if you have two companies of similar size, and one ranks highly and the other does not, you can tell that the second company is probably not very good to work for.

Business magazines like *Forbes* and *Fast Company* sometimes do reviews of companies, but they aren't always in the area in which you want to work. While you may find an online index so you can do the search from home, it still may be worth going to a library and spending half an hour digging through a few years' worth of back issues to find if they mention any firms in your target area. If you need help, talk to a reference librarian.

TECHNOLOGY

It is generally unwise to pursue a company specifically because it uses a technology you like. Technology changes quickly, and what companies use when you are interviewed may not be what they use when you are hired. However, if there is a specific technology that you love or wish to explore, it can be good to base your search on that. If it's a language like Haskell or Smalltalk, the market may be small, but you can get a good list of organizations to target from a user group. If it's a vendor-supplied technology like Sophos or Novell, you can often get a list by contacting the vendor and asking who their best partners are in the areas in which you are looking.

THE SHORT LIST

Once you have your list, put it into a spreadsheet and start ranking each company from 1 to 4, where 1 is "not much" and 4 is "a lot." Each row represents a particular organization and each column represents a category. Then, total your rows. This will identify the order in which you will approach your targets. Pick the top five as your short list.

You can, of course, go through the effort of weighting the columns if you like. If your personal number one pick doesn't make your short list, feel free to change things manually. This needn't be a rigorous process. However, if the company you want doesn't make the initial cut, consider why it happened and whether you may need to add a variable or two to accurately capture what matters to you.

EXAMPLE SHORT LIST

Table 5.1 Example Decision Table							
Organization	Size	Salary	Distance	R&D	Python	Perl	Total
Weyland-Yutani	3	4	3	4	4	1	19
Cyberdyne Systems	3	1	4	4	1	4	17
Blue Sun	1	4	1	3	1	1	11
Veidt Industries	2	2	4	1	4	1	14
Soylent Corp	1	1	3	1	1	4	11

In the example above, the primary concerns are size of company, expected salary, distance from home, how much research and development can be done, and which primary language is in use. Since a company either does or does not use a language such as Python or Perl, they either get all or no points for it. From the total, it is clear that Weyland-Yutani should be the first targeted firm, followed by Cyberdyne Systems.

CHAPTER 6

Initial Reconnaissance: Uncovering Seeds

Once you have a company picked to target, it's time to have some fun. However, there is one very strong caution that must first be made.

ETHICS

Ethics were discussed in the Introduction, but are addressed again here because the misuse of this information can be dangerous, both to the people you are investigating and to yourself.

The rest of this book is about intelligence gathering about companies and people that have not granted you permission to investigate them. The techniques comprising the remainder of the book focus on legal and ethical ways to use these tools. However, it is entirely possible for you to use these tools improperly. The burden is upon you to understand, before you start, what they do and how they could be misused. When ethical or moral lines are mentioned here, understand that the purpose is not to push the beliefs of the author or publisher onto you. Instead, the goal is to point out potential land mines. If a line is crossed and an employer finds out, it could cost you your job, result in legal action, or even get you banned from your industry. Because of this danger, please take the time to understand what they do and how they work before blindly playing with these tools.

The point of this process is to identify information that you can use to customize a pitch to your prospective employer. This can be as subtle as creating image references to a person's hobby or as blatant as building a business plan to specifically meet their needs. However, as you do this, you may find things you would rather not have known. You may learn details about the religious or political affiliations of your future boss or coworkers. You may learn about their relationship status and sexual orientation. You may find evidence of distasteful or illegal activity. Be aware that this could happen and look for warning signs to enable you to stop your search before it takes you somewhere you'd rather not go.

CONTINUAL REASSESSMENT

Do some thinking about where you want to work and what the people who work there might be like. While large firms can be quite diverse and accepting, that is not necessarily true of smaller firms. Some small companies function like families, some expect employees to share a religious framework, and others want people to be nothing more than automatons. Discovering that all the executive officers of a firm attend the same church or were all part of the same group at college might not matter to some people, but to others, it could be a significant enough finding to knock that company from the short list. Just like investing in the stock market, don't get so wrapped up in the idea of working for your target company that you ignore warning signs that crop up during the reconnaissance process. These warning signs are one of the reasons this process exists.

If you learn things that make you not want to work there, spend some time verifying them. If, in the end, it makes sense to move on to another target, do so.

TIME MANAGEMENT

Time is a critical factor. It's hard to know when to call a research task done, because there's always one more task that might give an incremental improvement. When doing reconnaissance, it can be even harder, because there's no obvious point where additional effort returns less and less useful data. Sometimes, when you're researching you can get a few hours into a project and hit a wall, then a few hours after that find a piece of information that you can leverage into an entirely new round of research. Other times, you hit a wall and that's the end of it—additional work garners no worthwhile results. Still other times, you can find fascinating information that has no direct value to the task at hand but distracts you for hours. Because of this, it is wise to determine how much time to spend on each research task before you start.

Many tools will be discussed in the rest of this book, but the most critical one is a timer. Kitchen timers or timer apps work well, since you can set them to count up or down. This gives you the choice to set a hard or a soft time frame around your research. When using a hard time frame, you pick a limit, such as one hour, to research a company on, say, Google. You set your timer to one hour in countdown mode, turn it on, and go. When it pings, you're done. This can be abrupt and disconcerting, but if time has a tendency to get away from you, it is a useful technique.

In contrast, a soft time frame would involve setting the timer to count-up mode and turning it on as you start your research. Then, whenever you get bored, you glance at your timer to see if you've put enough time into it yet. If you have trouble forcing yourself to stay on task, and frequently get distracted, a soft approach can be great to help you get things done.

GOOGLE

The first place to start, as one might expect, is with a search engine. However, it's important to go a little deeper than your standard generic search. A basic search uses keywords that return results. Odds are that you seldom need to go any further than the first few pages of results before you find what you need. This was not always so. Back in the days when Lycos and AltaVista ruled the search space, you had to understand Boolean search modifiers to get to what you needed. In the modern world, this is done with search modifiers or filters. This book cannot thoroughly explore all of the modifiers that exist, though wonderful references can be found in the Reference appendix. There definitely are some specific aspects of Google that are worth reviewing.

Web search is Google's classic search function. This is what you get if you go to google.com and just start searching. It gives you a relatively basic view of the web and is a good starting point, but you can't just stop there.

News search (news.google.com) can give you information as to how often the company you are targeting has been in the news and how it has been depicted. You can search not only on the company name, but also on the names of company officers and products. This can help arm you with information as to how they rank with respect to their competition and what business challenges they may be facing.

Maps search (maps.google.com) is useful for getting you directions to your interview, but you can also use it to find alternative addresses. Alternative addresses can be field offices, branches, or even employee-only entrances. These can then be fed back into the web search with a keyword of "meeting" to see if the company is hosting any user groups or related meetings that you could join. Attending such meetings can be a great way to network with current employees and learn things that can help you better target your approach.

Groups (groups.google.com) is surprisingly powerful, especially if you are pursuing a technical job. While Google is seemingly making efforts to replace Groups with Google + , this search still gives you access to forums and Usenet postings over many years. You can do people-focused searches for existing and former employees to see how they feel about their companies and what technologies they use and to get a general feel for their personalities. You can also use these posts to gather information such as email addresses and personal sites that can be used for further analysis.

Google Blog Search (www.google.com/blogsearch) can be used in a similar manner to explore what individuals are writing about. This is where you would plug in information found from earlier searches to dive into personal opinions and get to know what the people you're thinking about working with really care about.

Google's Patent Search (www.google.com/?tbm=pts) can provide insight into what a company or an individual within a company finds valuable enough to warrant protecting. Not all companies have patents, but if they do, you can learn about some inner workings of the business and prepare yourself to ask informed questions. Almost no one bothers to do this, so if you're the only candidate that does, you've immediately set yourself apart from the pack.

Finally, Google Code (code.google.com) is a search for different forms of publicly available source code. If you're pursuing a development or support job, you can search on product or developer names and get a sense of their coding style. As with a patent search, this helps you to ask very insightful questions.

BING

In general, Bing is less useful for this sort of targeted search. There are Social and News sub-searches that work somewhat like Google's. The

Bing events search (www.bing.com/events/search) is worth mentioning. By putting in any address, events relatively near that address are displayed. The quality of the search results is completely dependent on how well Microsoft has parsed the data, but this can be a useful first step to working your way into an event at your target company.

In general, Bing is far more useful if you wish to write your own tools to interact with its API, a task beyond the scope of this book. Most qualified results will be found with either Google or one of the other tools mentioned in this chapter.

ALTERNATE SEARCH ENGINES

There are several competing search engines to Google and Bing. They often do not have the depth or flexibility of the mainstream players, but it is often worth doing a quick search on each of them to see if they uncover alternate facets of your targets.

Yippy (search.yippy.com) is intended to be a family-friendly search, but its primary use for reconnaissance is its metadata remix capabilities. On running a search, you are presented with returned results, as well as a special pane on the left that shows suggested searches. This can help you find new keywords. It also gives you a list of sources and easy site filters so you can dive somewhat more deeply as you uncover information.

Ixquick (ixquick.com) places a high emphasis on privacy. Privacy is less important for this level of search than it might be in other areas of your life. For the purpose of reconnaissance, Ixquick searches multiple search engines and can give you a deeper view of aspects of the web than you get from other sites. For similar cross-search-engine searching, also consider Dogpile (www.dogpile.com).

Blekko (blekko.com) uses an "editorial" approach, much as Yahoo once did, to create inbuilt categorization. Its search capabilities are only better than the mainstream search engines if you happen to hit a category that has been editorialized, but you can get very insightful results if you do.

Yacy (yacy.net) is slightly different in that it is a distributed peer-to-peer search engine. To run it, you must download it and install it locally, then access it via a web browser. Once loaded, it's quite fast and, due to the distributed nature of the search, can show areas of the Internet that would otherwise be buried on the later pages of other search engines.

So.cl (so.cl) is a Microsoft social search project. It's highly experimental and may not always work. When it does, it's like a shortcut to trending topics, all shown on a single page. This may not be as useful for discovering data about a specific organization, but it can be great at finding useful information about issues that affect that organization.

Complete Planet (aip.completeplanet.com) attempts to search the "deep web," and claims over 70,000 custom databases that are typically not well-indexed by more general tools. Its use will be hit and miss depending on the type of job for which you are applying, but if the job is highly data-focused, it can be invaluable. It's good to use this for a quick search on the organization you are targeting, then use it later to dive deeper into specific issues facing your target organization.

Finally, Search Engine Guide (www.searchengineguide.com/search-engines.html) can help you find specific search engines by industry. Type in the general type of search for which you are looking, such as "Publishing," and it will return a list of search engines that specialize in that industry. Then, just open each search engine in its own tab and search through them.

QUICK REFERENCE

Once you've done some surface scans, it's time to start collecting your data. You are specifically looking for information about the target organization and that organization's products, customers, and employees. There are many ways to organize information. These range from mind maps to databases to target listing. For this purpose, what often works best is a simple text file. Open Notepad or TextEdit if you're using Windows or OSX, respectively. (If you're on Linux, you already know what to use.) If you wish to use another tool, feel free to adopt this format to whatever works for you.

There are also note-taking tools like OneNote and EverNote that integrate with the cloud. These are excellent tools, but remember that any tools with built-in sharing include an additional level of risk. A security flaw in the hosted component of such a tool can result in all of this sensitive information you've collected becoming public. It may not be your fault, but it would certainly be your neck on the line. The risk is yours to take. Consider whether the lack of features in the simpler tools is offset by the increased risk level of the more advanced tools.

Structure the file as shown below:

```
__Organization__ Quick Reference

Organization:
* Web Addresses:
* Physical Addresses:
* News

Products:
* Product 1:
* Product 2:
* Product 3:

Services:
* Service 1:
* Service 2:
* Service 3:

Customers:
* Customer 1:
* Customer 2:
* Customer 3:

Employees:
* Employee 1:
* Employee 2:
* Employee 3:
```

Figure 6.1 Quick Reference Template

See how the document is broken up into sections. The top section is general company information, followed by information about specific products, services, and customers. You could then fill this in from a set of basic searches. As an example, consider Elsevier, the company that owns the Syngress imprint. Suppose you wished to get a job at the firm. You'd start by filling in some information:

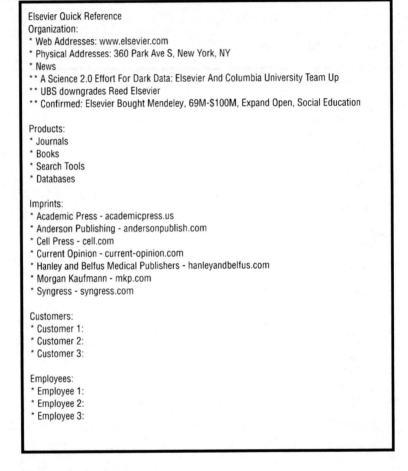

```
Elsevier Quick Reference
Organization:
* Web Addresses: www.elsevier.com
* Physical Addresses: 360 Park Ave S, New York, NY
* News
** A Science 2.0 Effort For Dark Data: Elsevier And Columbia University Team Up
** UBS downgrades Reed Elsevier
** Confirmed: Elsevier Bought Mendeley, 69M-$100M, Expand Open, Social Education

Products:
* Journals
* Books
* Search Tools
* Databases

Imprints:
* Academic Press - academicpress.us
* Anderson Publishing - andersonpublish.com
* Cell Press - cell.com
* Current Opinion - current-opinion.com
* Hanley and Belfus Medical Publishers - hanleyandbelfus.com
* Morgan Kaufmann - mkp.com
* Syngress - syngress.com

Customers:
* Customer 1:
* Customer 2:
* Customer 3:

Employees:
* Employee 1:
* Employee 2:
* Employee 3:
```

Figure 6.2 Elsevier Quick Reference

Note that, in this example, URLs are not used. This is a tradeoff between readability and speed. Anything that you find in searching can usually be found again. The goal of this document is to give you the ability to rapidly scan and remember information about the organization. You can track specific links as bookmarks or in another text file.

An exception is made for sub-brands (called "imprints" in the publishing field). A quick glance through the pages found for the basic search on Elsevier indicates that the firm has grown through acquisition and has kept the acquired entities as sub-brands. These brands have their own sites, and this information must be tracked to run additional searches through them.

FILLING IN THE LISTS

To fill in subsequent sections, you'll have to dig into search engine filtering. There are two major things you'll want to find out. The first is a list of employee names. This helps you determine at whom to target your job discussion and which individuals might be able to help you through the process. The second is the email address pattern that is used within the organization. Once you know these two things, you can create a list of names.

One way to start is to search on the organization's domain name but exclude hits that are on that actual domain. For the Elsevier example, this is difficult, as Elsevier has a lot of domains to filter out. A sample Google search would look something like this:

'"elsevier.com"   -site:elsevier.com-site:elsevierdirect.com-site:reedelsevier.com'

This search will find all references to elsevier.com in Google's database but exclude those references that come from sites like www.elsevier.com, ftp.elsevierdirect.com, and so on. The search string expands as you add more and more domains to exclude. However, this search alone, when run within the Google Groups interface, uncovers the following email addresses:

- Barranguet, Christiane (ELS-AMS) <C.Barr...@elsevier.com>
- Siebert, Mark (ELS-AMS) <M.Si...@elsevier.com>
- h.han...@elsevier.com
- m.malagutti@elsevier.com
- b.summ...@elsevier.com

It looks as though the pattern for email address creation is first initial, followed by a dot, then the last name of the person, at elsevier.com. Google makes this a bit more challenging by hiding part of the email address to hinder spammers. Luckily, it's not too hard to confirm. A quick search on "Barranguet, Christiane (ELS-AMS)" points to a mailing list at the University of Rhode Island. Like Google, this mailing list hides email addresses from nonsubscribers, but there's no barrier to subscribing. One "join" later, and you can read the email message in its entirety, seeing that Christine's email address is:

"Barranguet, Christiane (ELS-AMS)" <C.Barranguet@elsevier .com>.

Thus, the initial assumption is confirmed and the pattern is known.

Be careful about joining mailing lists to get information. In this case, there was no disclaimer or license statement that must be agreed to in order to gain access. If there had been, a deeper search to get possible email addresses would have had to have been done so there would be more to search on. In general, though, people tend to treat their email addresses as public data, making it fairly easy to find the pattern for most organizations. This technique will find email addresses that are posted as part of mailing lists or forums. It will not get you a complete list of employees, but since you are merely trying to verify a pattern, it works well.

Now that the pattern is known, it's time to build a list of individuals who work at the target organization. Some organizations are kind enough to publish their board of directors and their executives. A simple search on "Elsevier CEO" points us to www.elsevier.com/about/management. This gives a list of names which, if combined with the pattern previously identified, gives us some targets:

- Ron Mobed - Chief Executive Officer - R.Mobed@elsevier.com
- Youngsuk (Y.S.) Chi - Chairman - Y.Chi@elsevier.com
- David Lomas - Chief Financial Officer - D.Lomas@elsevier.com
- Gavin Howe - Executive Vice President, Human Resources - G.Howe@elsevier.com

- Bill Godfrey - Chief Information Officer and Head of Global Electronic Product Development - B.Godfrey@elsevier.com
- Adriaan Roosen - Executive Vice President, Operations - A.Roosen@elsevier.com
- Mark Seeley - Senior Vice President and General Counsel - M.Seeley@elsevier.com
- Eser Keskiner - Director of Strategy - E.Keskiner@elsevier.com
- David Ruth - Senior Vice President, Global Communications - D.Ruth@elsevier.com

If your target organization isn't kind enough to publish a list of people, check on company-reporting sites like crunchbase.com. You can further fill in the list by searching LinkedIn. LinkedIn, it turns out, has a business model quandary. On one hand, it wants to make its information hard to access, as the company's valuation is dependent, in part, on how connected people are. By making it harder to get data without being connected to people, LinkedIn encourages additional linking. However, it also wants to make it easy for its data to show up in search engine results. Thus, with a bit of filtering, you can get a nice list of names. Your first step is more likely to search on the term "elsevier" on the site linkedin.com. So the initial search on Google should be something like: "elsevier site:linkedin.com."

As you can see, this also lists businesses with "Elsevier" in the name, so further filtering is needed. The pattern in the URLs, though, is that people have /pub/ listed. Thus, you can further filter down to "elsevier site:linkedin.com inurl:pub" and get a list of people who apparently work at Elsevier. This can allow you to expand your people list:

- Rudy Wedenoja - Sr. VP Reed Elsevier Technology Services - R.Wedenoja@elsevier.com
- Michael Hansen - CEO, Elsevier Health Sciences - M.Hansen@elsevier.com
- Christopher Morrison - Editor-in-Chief, Biopharmaceuticals and Consumer Products at Elsevier Business Intelligence - C.Morrison@elsevier.com

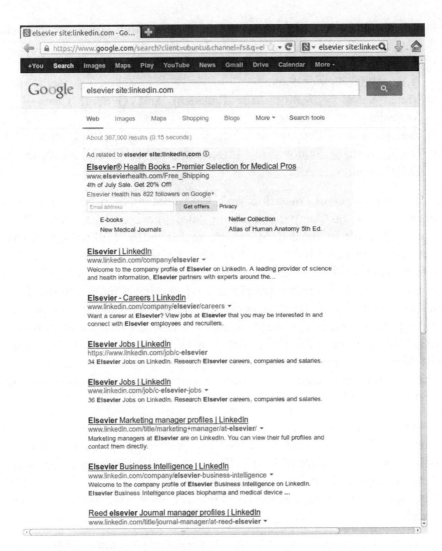

Figure 6.3 Basic Google/LinkedIn Search

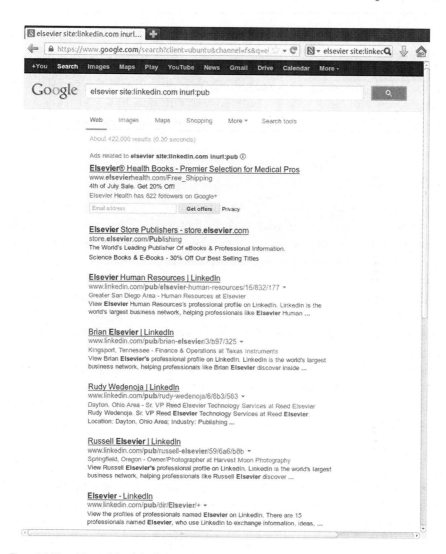

Figure 6.4 More Advanced Google/LinkedIn Search

Clearly, you can spend quite a lot of time digging through the results and building yourself a list. At this point, it may make sense to drill further down and focus on a subcompany of Elsevier, or a specific brand. The goal is to get a reasonably complete list of the people with whom you will be working—both so you can decide if you truly want to and to obtain a list of the people that might interview you.

HARVESTER

Sometimes a manual search of the Internet is too time consuming; you just want to launch a tool and look at the results. There are many tools that simplify this process for you, but beware: They can be dangerous. First of all, the more effective such tools are, the less people will use commercial search engines, so the search engine companies constantly fight to make this sort of scraping more difficult. This means that you cannot always rely upon the accuracy of the data returned. More importantly, however, some tools have active modes that can launch attacks directly against a company's infrastructure. Indirect data gathering is almost guaranteed to not be detected by a target. Direct data gathering can not only be noticed, but might be illegal, depending on where you live and where the target is located. One tool that is relatively safe to use is the Harvester.

The Harvester can be found at code.google.com/p/theharvester and is a fairly uncomplicated Python script. If you are running Linux or OSX, you likely already have Python. If you are running Windows, you may have to install it yourself. Installing Python on your system, if it is not already there, is outside the scope of this book—search for instructions specific to your operating system. Once that's done, you can run the Harvester against a target domain with ease:

```
$ python theHarvester.py -d elsevier.com -b all
**************************************
*TheHarvester Ver. 2.2 *
*Coded by Christian Martorella *
*Edge-Security Research *
*cmartorella@edge-security.com *
**************************************
Full harvest..
[ - ] Searching in Google..
    Searching 0 results...
    Searching 100 results...
[ - ] Searching in PGP Key server..
[ - ] Searching in Bing..
    Searching 100 results...
[ - ] Searching in Exalead..
    Searching 100 results...
    Searching 200 results...
[ + ] Emails found:
------------------
DecisionSupport@elsevier.com
custcare@elsevier.com
usmleconsult.help@elsevier.com
online.help@elsevier.com
b.issler@elsevier.com
s.cahill@elsevier.com
c.melis@elsevier.com
c.capot@elsevier.com
permissions@elsevier.com
jp.dls@elsevier.com
sales.inquiry@elsevier.com
internet@elsevier.com
usa@elsevier.com
i.internet@elsevier.com
commercialsales@elsevier.com
rachel.zaleski@elsevier.com
rh.jones@elsevier.com
t.reller@elsevier.com
virtualELibrary@elsevier.com
n.khan@elsevier.com
c.hurley@elsevier.com
[ + ] Hosts found in search engines:
-----------------------------------
```

```
207.24.42.81:store.elsevier.com
213.129.83.155:www.elsevier.com
54.243.180.71:evolve.elsevier.com
198.81.200.90:www.textbooks.elsevier.com
198.81.200.90:Textbooks.elsevier.com
198.81.200.138:books.elsevier.com
198.185.19.233:developers.elsevier.com
24.123.6.130:article20.elsevier.com
207.24.42.81:www.store.elsevier.com
145.36.215.180:ees.elsevier.com
207.24.42.81:Store.elsevier.com
198.81.200.138:www.books.elsevier.com
207.24.42.81:store.elsevier.com
213.129.83.155:www.elsevier.com
74.117.207.219:support.elsevier.com
54.243.180.71:evolve.elsevier.com
208.40.252.150:evolvels.elsevier.com
145.36.215.180:ees.elsevier.com
198.81.200.90:textbooks.elsevier.com
198.81.200.90:Textbooks.elsevier.com
198.185.19.233:www.developers.elsevier.com
[ + ] Virtual hosts:
= = = = = = = = = = = = = = = = = = =


207.24.42.81      store.elsevier.com
213.129.83.155     www.elsevier.com
54.243.180.71     evolve.elsevier.com
198.81.200.90     textbooks.elsevier.com
198.81.200.90     v5.books.elsevier.com
198.81.200.90     v5.textbooks.elsevier.com
74.117.207.219     support.elsevier.com
```

This data can then be added to your list for further reference. Other tools of this nature include eSearchy, eSearchy-ng, and eSearchy-mirai. At the time of writing this book, however, these eSearchy variants were not being maintained.

With any of these tools, it is extremely important to keep only the information you need to prepare yourself for the interview. As these tools are the same ones used by malicious attackers, the presence of the data could be used as evidence against you should a company take offense at your approach. Don't get greedy, keep your focus, discard anything you don't need, and you should be fine.

FILLING IN BY TITLE

Several tools exist to help you find people by title. They can be used to help determine the pool of potential interviewers. The classic way to do this is further LinkedIn mining. Using the searches referenced earlier, search the LinkedIn site and riff on brand names and job titles:

- "elsevier editor site:linkedin.com inurl:pub"
- "syngress editor site:linkedin.com inurl:pub"
- "elsevier 'project manager' site:linkedin.com inurl:pub"
- "syngress 'project manager' site:linkedin.com inurl:pub"

This can get you a decent list fairly quickly, but there are other options.

Market Visual

Market Visual (www.marketvisual.com) can be used to search on a company name and a title and will give you a list of possible targets. A search on "executive elsevier" provides a nice list of potential candidates. But it is very important to realize that all data is not equal. Consider the executive search that turns up an individual named Cornelis Josephus Antonius van Lede. That's a fairly distinctive name. A quick Google search turns up a long history in business, with a director position at Elsevier from 2003 to 2007.

Market Visual, however, lists him as holding a shocking 257 jobs at 44 different companies in the course of his career. This is theoretically possible, but it seems somewhat unlikely. Other hits from the same search indicate things like Strauss Zelnick with 216 roles at 65 firms, Lisa Hook with 138 roles at 35 firms, and Andrew Prozes with 104 roles in 30 firms.

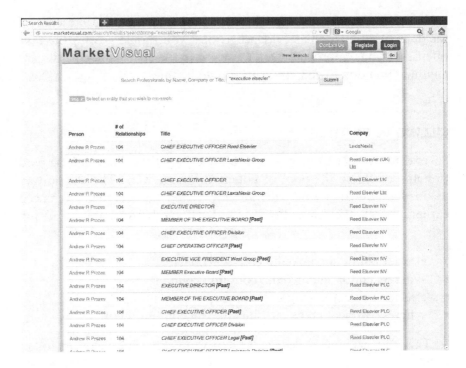

Figure 6.5 Market Visual

The lesson here isn't that some sites lie. This information could well be accurate. The lesson is that researching over 200 different jobs for a person with whom you may or may not interview is not an effective use of time. Some data sets are cleaner than others, and the effort it takes to adjust data sets could often be better spent on other parts of the process. If you feel that you are spending too much time on a specific task, feel free to make a note to come back to it once you know more.

If the opportunity warrants deep research, do it, just remember how much time an activity is worth.

Jigsaw/SalesForce Data.com Connect

Jigsaw (jigsaw.com) is a tool that is often used by sales professionals and recruiters to identify people in specific roles in target companies. It can be used much like Market Visual but doesn't go as deep. Jigsaw uses a point system, where the more data you input into the system, the more you can get out. This can take some time; though, as a result, the data set is often cleaner. Fortunately, when pursuing a job, you can find phone numbers fairly easily through Google or by calling an automated phone attendant, and it's fairly easy to guess at email addresses. Jigsaw can help you with first and last names and titles, which is all you really need for targeting.

Hoover's

Hoover's (hoovers.com) is a competitor to Jigsaw but is aimed more solidly at larger businesses. It uses the Dun & Bradstreet database, so all the data is quite clean. Though corporate access to this site can be quite expensive, there is a student edition that can be purchased for a monthly contract. At the time of writing, the cost was $50/month, which still might be excessive, depending on the role you are pursuing.

If you can get a decent list from sites like Google, LinkedIn, Market Visual, and Jigsaw, you're probably good. However, if you're targeting a particularly private company, it might be worth purchasing a one-month subscription to Hoover's. Then, once you have a reasonably complete list, you can move on to deeper reconnaissance.

THREAT AGENT

Threat Agent is a web-based tool focused on people who work in the information security field. Found at www.threatagent.com, this is a very easy way to collect basic analytics. The free version does not provide all results, but all results can be obtained for $10 per month. The basic version provides basic attack likelihood data, which you are unlikely to need, as you will (hopefully) not be directly attacking your targets. There is an asset map that does a good job of identifying geographical distributions of offices and individuals. It also lists servers and email addresses of people who work at your targeted organization. If you have difficulty running the more technical tools discussed above, this web-based tool may be a reasonable replacement.

RECON-NG

There is a new tool under active development that has the goal of replacing several of the independent reconnaissance tools under a standard framework. Called Recon-ng, this tool by Tim Tomes appears to be extremely promising—but at the time this book is being written, it is not yet sufficiently well-documented to be discussed. In an attempt to prevent this book from rapidly fading into obsolescence, it is mentioned here.

When you read this, visit the Recon-ng wiki at bitbucket.org/LaNMaSteR53/recon-ng/wiki/Home and see if the "Acquiring API Keys" section has more in it than "TBD" for each type of key. Once that is done, and if it is maintained, the Usage Guide in the wiki should be sufficient to guide you through the concepts discussed within this chapter.

CHAPTER 7

Deeper Reconnaissance: Uncovering Hidden Data

Now that you have a basic list, it's time to dig deeper. There are two types of digging that you will need to do. The first involves gathering more information about the company. This will involve mining the past and, if possible, projecting out into the future. The goal is to identify what challenges the business faces today, so you can position yourself to meet them tomorrow. Along the way, you want to try to identify what has been tried in the past, so you don't show up to the interview with tried and failed recommendations.

The second goal is to identify key information about the specific individuals who will be interviewing you. This is where the reconnaissance of individuals associated with a company will be important. The more complete your data and lists on these people, the better this part of the process will be.

COMPANY ANALYSIS

When analyzing a company, you must constantly question whether you want to work there. At this point in the analysis, you have enough data to begin answering the question. You must also consider whether the company will want you to work there. This is by no means certain. To gain a good job, you have to provide good value. This means that not only do they have to like you, but you also have to be able to show them that you can solve problems more cheaply or faster than anyone else they've interviewed. Gathering data is the first step to being able to do that, but decidedly not the last.

Determining Recent Finances

A successful organization will be more likely to hire you than one that is facing financial challenges. It can, however, be difficult to determine where your target organization sits. If it's a public company, you can look at stock performance on sites like Google Finance (www.google.com/finance) and Yahoo Finance (finance.yahoo.com).

You can also review recent documents from the SEC filings site (www. secinfo.com), though this may primarily be useful for US-based firms.

If the organization is a private company, you may wish to know what former employees have to say. Be careful, though. Some industries (governmental and military, for example) may consider this approach to cross an ethical line. If you decide to do this, though, you can easily use the LinkedIn search techniques discussed elsewhere in this book, identify employees who left the organization in the last two years, then contact them. Use short, to-the-point emails. Just ask them what it was like to work there, if they think it would be worth applying, and whether or not the organization's financial position is strong.

Some companies will be fine with former employees answering questions like "Did you enjoy working there?" and "What kind of work did you do?" but will be far more concerned with people asking about the financial position of the company. Instead of asking things like "Can you tell me about the company's financials?," consider phrasing questions like "Were you to take a job there now, would you be concerned about whether the job would last?" and "How likely is it that a cash flow problem would cause my projects to be canceled?"

Once you know where the organization fits on the financial growth spectrum, you can begin to determine whether to position their hiring of you as "support existing growth," "accelerate existing growth," or "help the company become profitable." This determination will help you frame your approach when you begin discussing the situation with them.

Analyzing the Present
By now, you should have a nice list of email addresses. Fortunately, this is all you need to begin identifying cultural issues. While there is nothing better than actually asking people what it's like to work at a place, there are tools you can use to get a general sense. One such tool is Rapleaf.

Rapleaf is a marketing company based on the concept that if you upload a list of email addresses, it will return a generalized view of what that group of people is like. It is intended to allow marketing professionals to upload a target list and then craft a marketing campaign around the age and income levels found to match the majority of the list. It also identifies information about political and religious affiliations, as well as average education, if that data is available. To access it, all you have to do is go to www.rapleaf.com, create a free account, and upload your list. Once it's processed, you'll have some general cultural data to review. Look for salary and political/religious information initially. If the average salary is low, you'll know going in that you might not get the offer you want. If the political or religious stances of the employees are at odds with yours, you may decide that you wouldn't fit in very well and decide to pursue a different organization.

Once you've reviewed that data and have a decent idea that you want to proceed, you may choose to conduct interviews. If you are brave, just reach out to some of the names on the list with a message like "I'd like to work for your company. Could you take a few minutes and help me understand what you need, so I can see if it makes sense for me to apply?" Most such emails will get no reply, but if even one person responds, that gives you more information to use as the process goes on.

If you want to maximize your success when sending these blind emails, remember the rule for the elevator pitch—make it about them. You've done a bit of research as to your target. Look for articles or blog posts they've made recently. Do some research around them and see if you can find something they missed. Start your email with something like "I read your article on <topic> and found it fascinating. It was somewhat reminiscent of <something else>. What are your thoughts on how <yet another thing> affects <topic>?" That shows that you're both interested and intelligent. Then you can move into your question with something like, "I've been meaning to contact you for a while. Your company sounds interesting and I was wondering what it was like to work there. Would you be willing to take a few minutes to help me understand what you need, so I can see if it makes sense to apply? I'd also be interested in talking more about <topic>, if that's of interest to you." This approach is a bit longer but much warmer. The risk, of course, is that you should be genuinely interested in the topic at hand and be able to engage in a discussion around it.

If you're not brave enough to contact people at the company directly, consider asking friends of yours to introduce you to people in similar positions as the people you'll be interviewing with. It's not hard to find people that match on critical characteristics. For example:

- CEO of a business with $5–$10 million in annual revenue
- CTO of a nonprofit organization with 10 direct reports
- Director of development for an organization using Agile development in .Net

Just go onto LinkedIn and start doing searches on common keywords to find someone worth talking to. Then look at your link map and ask whoever links you to them to set up an informational interview with them. This interview is not for a job but to help you understand what sort of things you need to be thinking about going into the interview you want to have. Many people in senior positions will gladly take an hour from their day to go out to lunch and discuss themselves and their needs.

Uncovering the Past

The idea behind researching the past is to make sure that you are aware of the events leading to an organization's present situation. If you spend too much time in this part of the process, you risk not only wasting your time but also learning too many of the wrong things, so set the timer for something reasonable, like four hours. Then, start digging in.

The first thing to check is that you have a reasonable list of domains to investigate. In the Elsevier example, there are additional imprints or brands that might need investigation, particularly if you wish to target your search on one of them. There could also be sites beyond just www on that domain. Some domains have ftp, www2, and webmail sites. Some larger firms have a great many of these sites, which can provide a lot of interesting information. While there are many ways to do this, including the incredibly powerful tool Maltego (explored later), a very fast way to do this is with a tool called Fierce.

Fierce is a Perl script that can be found at ha.ckers.org/fierce. If your system doesn't have Perl installed already, you'll need to do that, but once installed, running the script is remarkably simple. Just execute it with the search domain you're interested in. In most jurisdictions, running tools like this is not illegal, but it may be viewed as skirting an ethical line in more conservative industries.

Note: This example is abridged.

```
$ perl fierce.pl -dns elsevier.com
DNS Servers for elsevier.com:
    ns.elsevier.co.uk
    ns1-e.dns.pipex.net
    ns0-e.dns.pipex.net

Trying zone transfer first...
    Testing ns.elsevier.co.uk
    Request timed out or transfer not allowed.
    Testing ns1-e.dns.pipex.net
    Request timed out or transfer not allowed.
    Testing ns0-e.dns.pipex.net
    Request timed out or transfer not allowed.

Unsuccessful in zone transfer (it was worth a shot)
Okay, trying the good old fashioned way ... brute force
Checking for wildcard DNS...
Nope. Good.
Now performing 1895 test(s)...
198.81.200.85 about.elsevier.com
145.36.156.10 asia.elsevier.com
198.185.19.75 auth.elsevier.com
145.36.3.35 build.elsevier.com
198.81.200.85 careers.elsevier.com
145.36.3.35 ci.elsevier.com
145.36.211.114 cvs.elsevier.com
124.217.228.253 de.elsevier.com
206.137.74.251 delta1.elsevier.com
8.29.134.3 demo.elsevier.com
145.36.164.50 design.elsevier.com
198.185.19.233 developer.elsevier.com
198.185.19.233 developers.elsevier.com
198.81.200.85 earth.elsevier.com
198.81.200.139 ecommerce.elsevier.com
213.129.83.155 email.elsevier.com
206.137.75.26 ltolibrary.elsevier.com
206.137.75.21 hudson.elsevier.com
206.137.75.16 elsnycvclus01.elsevier.com
206.137.75.11 ns-esi.elsevier.com
206.137.75.10 madison.elsevier.com
206.137.75.12 bleecker.elsevier.com
206.137.75.13 nypinf1.elsevier.com
206.137.75.14 elsnycvexch01.elsevier.com
```

```
206.137.75.22 datatrax.elsevier.com
206.137.75.25 bills4si.elsevier.com
206.137.75.31 exch.elsevier.com
.
.
.
206.137.75.46 test1.elsevier.com
206.137.75.50 pluto.elsevier.com
206.137.75.51 neptune.elsevier.com
206.137.75.52 saturn.elsevier.com
206.137.75.53 jupiter.elsevier.com
206.137.75.54 mars.elsevier.com
206.137.75.55 usage.elsevier.com
206.137.75.56 eibackup.elsevier.com
206.137.75.59 venus.elsevier.com
206.137.75.31 exchange.elsevier.com
193.131.223.37 ftp.elsevier.com
145.36.214.103 ftp2.elsevier.com
145.36.214.150 gemini.elsevier.com
217.64.169.5 germany.elsevier.com
```

You can also add the "-search" flag to have it uncover other similar domains. When run with "-search elsevier," the search returned a massive set of elsevier.nl domains that were not directly useful. This tool tends to work better when used to find hosts on a domain than to find possibly related domains. It overlaps with other tools mentioned in this book, such as the Harvester, Maltego, and the various eSearchy versions. However, it seems to return a wider set of findings than other tools that are not directly focused on DNS.

If you have a higher-than-average level of technical skill, you may wish to try fierce2, available at trac.assembla.com/fierce. This tool has more dependencies and, therefore, is more difficult to install. However, it is more flexible and will uncover more data. If you are comfortable with the idea of installing additional Perl modules on your system, use fierce2. Otherwise, use the original tool.

Next, if you wish, you can directly access these resources. You may wish to consider running these checks through some sort of anonymizing proxy or VPN service. In most areas of the world, there's nothing wrong with just visiting a website, but in some places and industries, you may need to exercise more caution. Remember, if the risk is more than you are comfortable with, just skip this phase entirely. You may not obtain as much data to inform your approach, but you'll certainly be safer from organizations that might blacklist you from being hired or take action against you, should you be detected.

If you wish to explore using anonymizers, be aware that the best option for any specific need changes rapidly as the people who write the tools engage in an arms race with the organizations that wish to defeat them. Do your own research on "OpSec" or "Operational Security" before starting. Tools like Tor and services like Hide My Ass! (hosted vpn) are popular at the time of this book's writing.

Once you have the list of hosts on each domain that warrants investigation, visit each one in a browser. As you review sites, look for sites that give you useful data. These sites often include names like "backup" or "test," or have numbers after the name. This indicates that you may be able to access legacy or not-yet-launched sites. The goal is to build a list of useful sites; ignore the rest. Basically, you're weeding out the ones that aren't worth spending any more time on.

●●●──

Legal Concerns

As you investigate these sites, be very careful about access warnings. A good example is at the site ftp://ftp.elsevier.com. If you pull this site up in a browser, you'll see a README.TXT file there. If you open the file, you'll see a warning at the bottom:

```
-------------------------------------------------------------------------------
  LEGAL NOTICE
  ----------------------------
```

This system is for the use of authorized users only. Individuals using this computer system without authority, or in excess of their authority, are subject to having all of their activities on this system monitored and recorded by system personnel.

In the course of monitoring individuals improperly using this system, or in the course of system maintenance, the activities of authorized users may also be monitored.

Anyone using this system expressly consents to such monitoring and is advised that if such monitoring reveals possible evidence of criminal activity, system personnel may provide the evidence of such monitoring to law enforcement officials.

Since it is highly unlikely that you count as an "authorized" user, this is an example of a site that should be avoided. If you feel you absolutely must visit such a site, protect yourself by browsing anonymously, but be aware of the risk that you are taking.

Once you have your list of sites, the next place to go is the Internet Archive's Wayback Machine (archive.org/web/web.php). Just paste in the URL of each site you care about and look at older versions of those sites. You can learn a lot about how the company has evolved over time by looking at how the site has changed. As seen in this example, www.elsevier.com has been archived 1,315 times, going back to 1996. There was a lot of change happening in 2005.

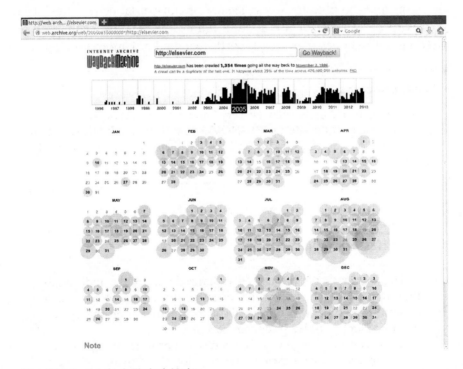

Figure 7.1 Internet Archive's Wayback Machine

By reviewing how Home, About, and Contact pages change, you can get a feeling for what has been important to an organization over time. For example, in the first Syngress archive, back in 1998, the company focused on publishing networking books. As time went by, the focus moved to test preparation, then to security—and eventually it was acquired by Elsevier, which focuses more generally on scientific knowledge, of which security is a component.

Build a basic timeline to better understand specific events that affected your target company. This can be added to later. You can also use press releases to fill in specific details. The site www.prweb.com can be used to search press releases and map events to specific dates.

Example Timeline for Elsevier:

- 1996
  - Focused on science, specifically chemistry, medicine, computers, economics, and mathematics
- 1998
  - Site change, more of a global focus
- 2000
  - Launched "browse our journals" feature
  - Changed focus to general science
- 2002
  - Focus on scientific, technical, and medical information
- 2004
  - Language changed to being a "partner" to the scientific, technical, and health communities
- 2005
  - Adjusted site to focus on authors, editors, and librarians … user focus
- 2006
  - Added "for societies" to focus
  - Acquired Syngress publishing
  - Added "Elsevier Websites" link for sub-branding
- 2008
  - Acquired Edra S.p.A.
  - Acquired Professional Development Software, Inc.
- 2009
  - Site redesign
  - Highlighting new journals and acquisitions
  - Acquired William Andrew Publishing
- 2010
  - Site redesign
  - Featuring different products/brands
  - RSS shown prominently

- 2011
  - Acquired Oncology Journal Portfolio
  - Acquired Fisterra.Com
- 2012
  - Site redesign
  - Focus on librarians, health practitioners, industry research, academia, and government
  - RSS less prominent but still there

This rough timeline can be filled in and mapped to when your prospective coworkers and interviewers joined the company, so you have some idea as to what changes they've seen.

Finally, since this particular target has an RSS feed of its press releases (www.elsevier.com/press-releases), you can subscribe to the feed and be up-to-date with respect to changes within the company as you approach the interview process. Smaller companies won't have a press release feed but may have Twitter or blog feeds that can be followed instead. Following near-real-time data feeds is much like looking through the archives. Just check the new items and keep the timeline updated with more recent events.

Discovering the Future

While it is not possible to foresee the future with anything close to accuracy, you do not need high levels of accuracy to land a job. The point of looking toward the future is to understand enough about the challenges facing your target to start coming up with solutions. No one expects you to be able to actually implement them before you've worked at your target organization for a while, but the fact that you've put thought into the process will set you apart from other applicants.

Some guesses about what the organization is planning can be surmised from press releases and trends seen in the timeline. What direction is the organization moving? Is it focusing more on customers or on investors? Is it trying to move faster or is it shedding unnecessary work and refocusing on the core business? Is the primary market full? If so, is it trying to branch into new markets or trying to take over market share from other companies? If it's a public company, how has the stock been doing? How has the stock of its competitors performed?

You can support some of these guesses by looking at industry research. Companies that are in the top three in their respective categories are often as big as they're going to get in their current markets until a competitor stumbles. If everything's been stable for several years, odds are that the target company is looking at other markets. Blog posts, press releases, new products and services, and website changes will help illustrate what those markets are.

For deeper analysis, you'll need to use some tools. A good one to start with is Google Trends (www.google.com/trends). Remember, you're venturing into the realm of uncertainty here, so consider carefully what the results tell you. To extend the Elsevier example, here is a Google Trends search on the word "publishing."

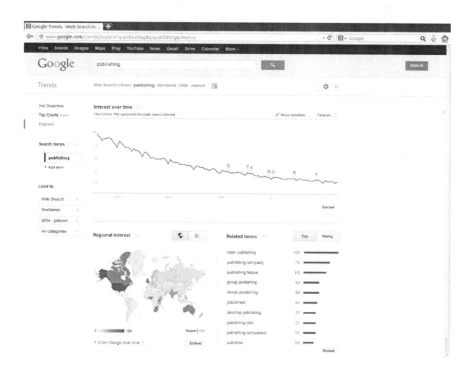

Figure 7.2 Google Trends – Publishing

As you can see, publishing is decreasingly discussed on the Internet as time goes by. Phrases like "book publishing" and "book publishing jobs" show a similar downturn. This can indicate a shrinking industry. However, bear in mind the shifts that were evident on Elsevier's website over time. The most recent redesign showed a focus on librarians, health practitioners, industry research, academia, and government. Consider this search on "research library," as that seems to be a direction in which Elsevier is heading.

Figure 7.3 Google Trends--Research Library

Note that this is less of a downward slope; but more interestingly, there is strong regional interest. In addition to the US and Canada (common hits when searching on English terms), there is also interest in this term in India, Australia, New Zealand, and, surprisingly, the Philippines, South Africa, and Nigeria. These unexpected hits could indicate an emerging market around which the company could focus. A search on "government research" indicates a similar country breakdown.

There are other trending features of sites like Yahoo, Bing, and Twitter, but those are less interactive and more focused on letting you know what's trending right now rather than how things have historically trended over time. They're good if you want to boost your awareness in a more general way but less useful for targeting a company.

For more detailed analytics, check out newcomers like Recorded Future (www.recordedfuture.com) and Silobreaker (www.silobreaker.com). These sites take more effort to learn and, at the time of this writing, do not have much reach, so the analytics are somewhat limited, but they're worth putting an hour or so into to see if their coverage overlaps with your needs. At the time of this writing, these sites had "basic" or "trial" free options, but there is no guarantee that will continue forever.

PROFESSIONAL ANALYSIS

Analyzing people is a different matter from analyzing organizations. At this point, your focus should be on who you want as your new boss. Remember, you're looking for a job that may not have been posted or even exist yet. You have to look for people with whom you'd work well. This requires having a decent feel for who works at the target organization and in which role. In a small business, you may be able to map out the entire organization. For large firms, this is not possible, so focus on the department or business unit in which you want to work. Attempt to figure out who your boss might be and what his or her team looks like. This is where the most powerful tool in the entire process comes in.

Maltego by Paterva may be found at www.paterva.com/web6/products/maltego.php. It is a downloadable Java application that comes in both commercial and free variants. The commercial version is available, at the time this book was written, for $650 for a one-year subscription. If you're currently employed and looking for a better job, you can do far worse than invest in this tool, as the commercial version allows you to search much more quickly. If you're not currently employed, you have a bit more available time, so the Community version will likely suffice. In either case, it is wise to start with the free Community version and get a feel for it first

Once you launch Maltego, you will be presented with either a "run a machine" dialog box or a blank graph, depending on the version you're running. The "machines" are nothing more than scripted searches, but can save you a bit of time. You can do the same work yourself by creating objects and then searching through the "transforms."

A transform, in Maltego, is a series of searches that can run from an object. For example, if you create a domain object, like "elsevier.com," you can right-click and choose to get all DNS entries for it, get email addresses, find files or documents, etc. Each of these searches will return additional objects that can then be searched in turn. As you search further and further, you will find more and more data. This is good for basic company searches, but we're also interested in people.

You have a list of email addresses that you've created, so this is where you start importing them. If you're relatively nontechnical, you can just copy and paste until they're all in, but if you're comfortable with getting your hands a bit dirty, it's relatively easy to create an XML file from your email address list and import it directly. To see the format, just manually create a few email addresses in Maltego, save the file as XML, then extend it.

From there, you can dig into each email address and try to match it to mailing lists, forums, websites, and social media entities. As you fine-tune your team list, you can narrow it down to a specific group of people and begin to get very specific. As you find information, bounce between digging further into Maltego and doing searches on social media sites like LinkedIn, Facebook, Twitter, and Google + . Depending on the age of the target and where they live, it may be worthwhile to search Internet archives for MySpace, Orkut, and Friendster. As you do, build out your list of personal data. Here's an example, again using Elsevier:

Ron Mobed - Chief Executive Officer - R.Mobed@elsevier.com
- Bloomberg Profile: http://investing.businessweek.com/research/stocks/private/person.asp?personId = 20594554
- LinkedIn: http://www.linkedin.com/profile/view?id=522564
  - Member: Association of Learned and Professional Society Publishers (ALPSP)
  - Member: Top Leaders/Executives
- Facebook: None
- Google Groups: References to oil usage and the Gulf War

Youngsuk (Y.S.) Chi - Chairman - Y.Chi@elsevier.com
  • LinkedIn: http://www.linkedin.com/profile/view?id=10131484
    • Member: Princeton Class of 1982
    • Member: Asian American Alumni Association of Princeton (A4P)
    • Member: Tools of Change for Publishing
  • Facebook: https://www.facebook.com/youngsuk.chi
  • Google Groups: Link to interview in the Economist

David Lomas - Chief Financial Officer - D.Lomas@elsevier.com
  • LinkedIn: www.linkedin.com/profile/view?id=118739673
    • Member: Notum Network

Gavin Howe - Executive Vice President, Human Resources - G.Howe@elsevier.com
  • LinkedIn: http://www.linkedin.com/profile/view?id=80177519,
    http://uk.linkedin.com/pub/gavin-howe/22/a27/3b

Bill Godfrey - Chief Information Officer and Head of Global Electronic Product Development - B.Godfrey@elsevier.com
  • LinkedIn: http://www.linkedin.com/profile/view?id=11526251
    • Member: Bank of America Employees & Alumni Network
    • Member: CIO Committee
    • Member: CIO Leadership Network - CIO Executive Summit
    • Member: Friends of The Hartford (1100+)
  • Google Groups: Many references, sort later

Adriaan Roosen - Executive Vice President, Operations - A.Roosen@elsevier.com
  • LinkedIn: http://www.linkedin.com/profile/view?id=4674005
    • Member: People Connected - Board and Executive Level Network

Mark Seeley - Senior Vice President and General Counsel - M.Seeley@elsevier.com
  • LinkedIn: http://www.linkedin.com/profile/view?id = 16596255
    • Member: Association of Corporate Counsel
    • Member: OnCopyright 2012
    • Member: STM publishing industry

Eser Keskiner - Director of Strategy - E.Keskiner@elsevier.com
  • LinkedIn: http://www.linkedin.com/profile/view?id = 1133509
    • Member: McKinsey & Company Alumni (Unofficial McKinsey Group)
    • Member: McKinsey entrepreneur
    • Member: STM Publishing Group
    • Member: Wharton Entrepreneurs & VCs
  Possibly related to the Cyprus Action Network: www.cyprusaction.org, investigate further

David Ruth - Senior Vice President, Global Communications - D.Ruth@elsevier.com
- LinkedIn: http://www.linkedin.com/profile/view?id = 19325236
- Member: Centre for Corporate Public Affairs
- Member: Corporate Communications Executive Network
- Member: International Government Relations and Public Affairs
- Member: Professional & Scholarly Publishing (PSP) Division
- Member: Reed Elsevier

The LinkedIn group membership information shows what interests the individuals have and, if the group is public, allows you to join and read discussions. Similar to this is Google Groups, where you can go and read a considerable amount of past communication. This communication can include specifically created Google groups, but also includes legacy Usenet groups that were used extensively before the advent of the World Wide Web.

Generally, the older a person is and the less technically focused they are, the less of a trail they will have on social media—but there might be more information available in public interviews. It can take a while to find them, but it can be done by searching on the person's name coupled with each company they worked for and the terms "interview" and "profile." Thus, to find articles on Ron Mobed, you would run the following searches on Google:

- "Ron Mobed" "Argus Media" interview
- "Ron Mobed" "Elsevier" interview
- "Ron Mobed" "Cengage Learning" interview
- "Ron Mobed" "IHS" interview
- "Ron Mobed" "Schlumberger" interview
- "Ron Mobed" "Argus Media" inurl:article
- "Ron Mobed" "Elsevier" inurl:article
- "Ron Mobed" "Cengage Learning" inurl:article
- "Ron Mobed" "IHS" inurl:article
- "Ron Mobed" "Schlumberger" inurl:article
- "Ron Mobed" "Argus Media" profile
- "Ron Mobed" "Elsevier" profile
- "Ron Mobed" "Cengage Learning" profile
- "Ron Mobed" "IHS" profile
- "Ron Mobed" "Schlumberger" profile

For younger people, there will be more of a trail on sites like Facebook, Twitter, and Google + . As social media changes over time, the specific sites will change, but general presence likely will not. Be sure to check out profiles, public posts, and lists of friends. Any friends' pages that contain public information could also leak useful information if you care to go digging further.

PERSONAL ANALYSIS

There's more to the Internet than Facebook. Some people disclose information on older social networking sites such as MySpace and LiveJournal. If you can map them to niche sites, you can learn even more. This process can get technically tricky and can sometimes drift into getting more personal than you like. If you can find a person's username, often from a Facebook or Twitter search, you can then search on that username and start following them throughout the web. Since people tend to try to keep the same usernames on numerous websites, it's fairly easy to develop a personal profile.

As an example, I chose the online name "guppiecat" as being globally unique a great many years ago. A search on that term uncovers the following online presences, and many more:

- Flickr
- LiveJournal
- Dreamwidth
- Scribd
- eBay
- WordPress
- daGur.us
- Technorati
- CyanogenMod

This was a deliberate choice to boost SEO, but a significant amount of information can be found for people even if they are not attempting to improve their personal visibility.

Beware though—there are some things you may not wish to know about your future employer or coworkers. You may wish to avoid following links to sites referencing sexual content, such as FetLife. Depending on your own sensitivities, you may also wish to avoid political, religious, and news forums and other hot-button topics.

In addition to searching with your favorite search engine for usernames, you can also use NameChk (namechk.com) to run a query for a specific name. If you want more control, or if that site is experiencing issues, consider Chris John Riley's Scythe tool (github.com/ChrisJohnRiley/Scythe). This is another Python script that, when pulled down with Git, is simply run as "./scythe.py –account = <account name>." You can optionally run it against a list of usernames if you want to cast a wider net.

When run against the same "guppiecat" username, Scythe found more sites that warrant investigation:

```
$ ./scythe.py –account = guppiecat
[X] Account guppiecat exists on flickr.com (Username)
[X] Account guppiecat exists on last.fm (Username)
[X] Account guppiecat exists on Github.com (Email)
[X] Account guppiecat exists on Yahoo (yahoo.com email)
[X] Account guppiecat exists on Yahoo (yahoo.co.uk email)
[X] Account guppiecat exists on GMail (username)
[X] Account guppiecat exists on myspace.com (Username)
[X] Account guppiecat exists on mahalo.com (Username)
```

●●●

Sensitive Data

It is unlikely you will find any need for any of the classic stalker data, such as age, ethnicity, home address, home value, etc. However, sites like PeopleFinders and Spokeo often come up on searches, so they must be addressed.

In general, you should be able to find all the data you need without resorting to paying anyone. Most of the "people search" sites are constructed to provide you with basic data for free and lure you into paying a small amount of money for "full" access; but there is no way to know how good the data is until after you pay.

A good rule of thumb is "If you don't need the data, don't pay for it." So think about the data you need before you start searching.

HAIL MARY SITES

There are far too many sites to explore each and every one that could be useful in this sort of reconnaissance process. There are a handful of sites that usually turn up little to no data, but when they hit, they hit big. This short section lists some sites you may wish to consider if there is additional time remaining in your research process. Just remember to stick to your preallocated research time. It's easy to waste a lot of time on tools like these.

LittleSis

LittleSis (littlesis.org) is intended as a social whistleblowing site like WikiLeaks. Unlike WikiLeaks, this site focuses on personal interaction and tends to include data about politically active individuals, especially Americans and people with links to Americans. If a person has an entry, you can expect to find a listing of political positions held, education and family relationships, important friends, and financial donations. The "Interlocks" tab is one of the most interesting. This shows people who are connected to the target and how. It's more transparent than sites like LinkedIn and easier to leverage.

Since most people on the site wield a fair amount of political power, they are harder to access, so the increased leverage may not get you much. However, if you are targeting a politically active individual, this can be a great way to find out what causes they support so you can alter your approach accordingly. Alternatively, if you have strong objections to these causes, you may wish to stop your efforts involving this organization and find a new target that better meets your needs.

Donations

OpenSecrets.org and FollowTheMoney (www.followthemoney.org) are also political sites, but they track donations instead of power. Few people donate money in sufficient quantities to get listed, but if one of your targets does, it can tell you a lot about their political beliefs. That said, there is a bias in favor of conservative organizations within business, as such organizations tend to support taxation models that are more attractive to business owners. So a donation to a candidate may indicate a financial perspective rather than a social one.

Also, be aware that many donations are given under legal names, so when searching, be certain to convert any nicknames to full names and experiment with trying middle names and initials if they are known. Often, it is easiest to search only on the target's last name, then manually sort through the list to see if they are included. You can also search on the company's name to see if the target organization itself has backed any candidates.

Social Mention

Social Mention (socialmention.com) attempts to track a target's social activities. As with many data mining sites, the quality of the data returned will be highly erratic. A search on exact name is required, since otherwise, first and last names are searched individually. As with other searches, globally unique usernames tend to work better than more common names. If your target has an active online video presence, this search will uncover highly useful information. However, for most hiring managers, the likelihood of that is low.

This site is included because as existing younger employees rise to positions of greater power, these sorts of niche social searches will become more useful.

NNDB Mapper

The NNDB Mapper (mapper.nndb.com) provides graphical representations of the data stored in NNDB (nndb.com). This site serves as a repository for information about noteworthy individuals. It is unlikely that the people who will be interviewing you will be sufficiently noteworthy to be listed, but it's worth checking, just in case. This site can list different groups with which they are affiliated, as well as the types of links they have to those groups.

Entity Cube

Entity Cube (entitycube.research.microsoft.com) is a project by Microsoft intended to improve the quality of search results for people rather than concepts. It is relatively new and highly experimental. Results vary day-to-day and sometimes stay static for quite a long time. Because it is a people-focused project with significant funding, it can sometimes return surprisingly useful results.

Wolfram Alpha

Wolfram Alpha (www.wolframalpha.com) is an attempt to reconceive how web searches are done. Its true power is in math and science searches; however, when searches are run against some companies or people, you can get very interesting visualizations of the available public data. This is not likely to be useful for small companies or specific departments, but if you need additional information on large firms and general trends, the data returned can be quite useful.

Glassdoor

Glassdoor (www.glassdoor.com) is basically a company review site. Just as you can get reviews of restaurants before you visit, at Glassdoor you can get reviews of organizations that tell you what it's like to work there, whether the salaries are comparable, and, if you're lucky, some of the interview questions asked. Not all companies are reviewed on GlassDoor and, for those who are, you must always remember that there are bad reviews and there are bad reviewers. Companies on sites such as this tend to attract a disproportionate number of bad reviewers, because the people who are happy in their jobs are often too busy to write up a review of their experience. Use Glassdoor to get some additional insight into your target organization, but remember that reviews are entirely subjective and that companies change over time. Older reviews should be given less credence.

CHAPTER 8

Metaphor Mapping: Adjusting to Your Target

Once you've found the people and have identified how they function within their organization, it's time to figure out how they and their organizations think. The way organizations think of themselves metaphorically has been explored in great detail in Gareth Morgan's excellent book *Images of Organization*. Within the context of a job search, it is important to understand that the people with whom you are interviewing have their own concepts as to what they need and what you'd be doing. These concepts are formed from several places, but at their core is the fact that metaphors are formed by, and in turn shape, the language used within an organization. Fundamentally, a metaphor can be thought of as one concept standing for another concept. Thus, if you are interviewing at an organization that prizes speed over all else, you'll see and hear language around things like workflow, downtime, delivery time, etc. Organizations focused on quality will discuss testing and best practices. Organizations that think of themselves as organisms will talk about resource constraints and growth over time. Additionally, different departments will have their own metaphors. Industry metaphors abound. The financial industries tend to discuss things in terms of growth and risk, and internal accounting groups adopt this language and way of thinking. Entrepreneurial fields also look at risk, but in a much more positive manner. Executives who come from entrepreneurial backgrounds tend to adopt this mode of thought. Groups that work with customers tend to focus on internal and external pain and shy away from activities that could create pain. Thus, quality assurance and internal support groups will use metaphors of certainty and avoidance.

People also use metaphors of their generation, hobbies, and cultural backgrounds. Sports metaphors are particularly common in business, where phrases like "we don't need a home run, we just need a lot of singles" and "move the project down the field" are common. To maximize success, it is wise to understand how your targets think. Metaphors are one good way to do this.

DISCOVERING EXISTING METAPHORS

If you can find what your targets have said or written, your task will be much easier. It will take some effort to find metaphors in other people's work, but it can be done. Using the techniques discussed in the Reconnaissance chapters, first, read what they said. It's important to understand the overall concept before you go to the next piece, looking at not just what they said but how they said it. Look first for similes. These are easy because they use the words "like" or "as," so you can just search in the text for those words. Each time they come up, think about the phrase and see if it is a technical comparison (a Ford Taurus is like a Honda Accord) or an imaginative one (a Ford Taurus is like a bull). In the latter case, you may have a metaphor.

Identify all possible metaphors, then reread the work. If the concept is extended in a meaningful way, such as, "A Ford Taurus is like a bull: it's strong and rugged—and if you drive it through a china shop, you'll break a lot of things," you have a metaphor. If it is not extended, it may still be of use, but it indicates that your target hasn't given that concept a lot of thought, so it won't be as useful as if he or she had.

Once you've built a list of metaphors for that work, look at other things your target has written or said and see if any metaphors recur throughout his or her career. If they do, you've won. Research as much of that concept as you can. For example, if he or she uses baseball metaphors constantly, become conversant in baseball before you go in for the interview. You don't have to get into the major leagues, but you should be able to read articles from ESPN.com and understand most of what is said. In general, five evenings is sufficient to build up an understanding and vocabulary to match your target. This increases your chances of "clicking" with your interviewer.

GUESSING AT METAPHORS

If you can't find metaphors in active use, you'll have to guess at them from stereotypes. Stereotyping can be dangerous but also quite useful. Just always keep in mind that you *are* stereotyping and could be wrong.

Industry

As mentioned before, industries have common metaphors. You probably know the metaphors of the industry you're going into. It can also be useful to understand the metaphors used in the industries in which your targets have worked. For example, if you are pursuing a job in health care, you will encounter people using concepts like the following:

- We have to keep the business healthy! (wellness)
- We must protect our clients! (safety)
- Buying our product is like a vaccine, it'll keep bad things from happening later. (medicine)

If you are going after a job in the financial sector, you'll see things like this:

- It's too risky to invest in that idea right now. (profit/loss)
- This product will help you improve quarter to quarter! (reporting)
- How will this affect our bottom line? (profit/loss)

You can often get a nice list of industry-specific metaphors by just doing a search on " <industry name> metaphors." If this does not return an immediate list, look for interviews with leaders in that industry. Go through the metaphor discovery process in the preceding section to find the common metaphors used in that industry. Go through each industry your probable interviewers have been active in, and spend sometime thinking about how they have been trained to think.

Generation

Generations of people experience events differently. In the United States, when planes struck the World Trade Center on 9/11/2001, it was devastating to younger people and inspired many of them to enter military service. To adults who had lived through earlier terrorist bombings or wars, such as Vietnam, Korea, or World War II, the event had much less impact. Though stereotyping people based on age has some significant risks, it is important to realize that older people often have less familiarity with technology (though this can vary by industry). Thus, phrases like "let's hit Undo and go over that again" are going to work less well than "let's page back a bit."

People who, when given the word "impeach," think of Johnson or Nixon, are very different from those who think of Clinton. They will likely conceive of political power very differently. People who never experienced divorce when they were growing up will think of family in quite a different way from people who grew up with multiple sets of parents and whose friends were in a similar position.

However, an attempt to appropriate another generation's metaphors without understanding them will fail completely. This failure to bridge a generational divide is at the core of jokes. A classic example can be seen on sitcoms where a parent born in the 1950s tries to connect with a child by using 1970s slang like "Just give me the skinny, I can dig it." However, if the child never lived through a time when that language was common, they only know it through ridiculous parody, so the phrase has the exact opposite effect as intended.

The way you phrase your ideas must take these differences into account. Try practice interviews with older or younger friends or those people's parents or children. Explain to them what you want to do for your target company and ask them to repeat it back to you in their own words. If they have difficulty doing this, ask them to compare it to something. Track how they do this. In general, younger people are more liberal, more familiar with technology, and more likely to reference consumer technology in their explanations. They will use phrases like "help grow the company like Google and Facebook did" and "do something that can go viral." Older people are more likely to use references to family, duty, and classic conservative values. They will use phrases like "help the company refocus on what really matters" and "do things that people will talk about."

Taking the time to understand what people have gone through, how they think about it, and what sorts of historical frameworks they use will help you connect with them. Additionally, taking this one step further and trying to figure out how to communicate with them in their own language will shrink any generation gap and make your discussion far more successful.

Hobbies

Another rich source of metaphor is hobby. People who knit, who play golf, or who do photography all have their own languages. Hobbies are listed on many social media platforms and are evident in interviews and photos. It generally takes very little research to identify the things your targets like to do in their off-hours. While some executives' primary hobby is making money, most people have one to three things about which they are passionate. Once you can identify that, you can start working with it.

Most hobbies give up their metaphorical secrets with a simple search on " <hobby> metaphors." Others you may need to pick up on yourself. Fortunately, the Internet is a gold mine for this sort of thing. Watch "getting started" videos on YouTube and find online forums and mailing lists to read. Learn a decent amount about the hobby so you can make a reference or two in your interview and portfolio material. If asked about it, say something like "I've really just started getting into it" or "It's interesting, but I've never had the time to dive as deep as I'd like." This will explain your lack of expertise without making it look like outright manipulation.

Of course, it's always possible you might find it fun and get far more into it than you ever expected. There's nothing wrong with this, but keep in mind that hobbies are intended to consume your time in an enjoyable manner. Time spent on a hobby does not directly advance your goal of getting a new job. By all means, have your fun, but keep your ultimate goal in mind.

Race and Culture

There is a ton of metaphor in race and culture. Ignore it all. Nothing sours a relationship faster than misusing another culture's metaphor, causing you to be viewed as classist or racist. Expert social engineers and diplomats can get away with this. Odds are, you can't.

While little in this book is about playing it safe, play it safe here. The risk of getting it wrong is extremely high, as is the cost of failure.

CHAPTER 9

Repositioning: How to Make You Stand Out

Until now, the search burden has been on you. It is quite reasonable to presume that any prospective employer will also invest some time into searching on you. It is unlikely that they will do it as deeply or effectively as you will have done by now. You must still address this area. First, clean up your online presence; then start boosting it.

REBOTTLING THE GENIE

Though there is a general view in many HR departments that researching prospective employees via social media is to be avoided, an ongoing Career Builder survey run by Harris Interactive in early 2013 reports that many of them do. In fact, between the 2012 and 2013 surveys, the number of hiring managers that do this sort of research increased by almost a fourth, with 43% of people admitting to rejecting candidates for several reasons, including:

- Posting of inappropriate photos and information
- Drug and alcohol use
- Sharing of negative information about employers
- Poor communication skills
- Racist, sexist, and other negative comments
- Lying

The same survey showed that positive information found from a similar search, ranging from professionalism to illustrating professional skills to showing a fuller picture of one's personality, including creativity and outside interests, can make it more likely to receive an offer.

It is often stated that anything done on the Internet is there for all time. This is somewhat true. However, we do view the Internet through different lenses. Typically, we call these lenses "Google" and "Bing," but there are others as well. The most thorough way to purge unnecessary items from your Internet presence is to follow all of the steps for researching a prospective employer, but do it on all variations of your own name. Anything you find that makes you look like a poor employee should be removed.

Then, visit each of your social media and search platforms and review your privacy settings. While there are far too many to list here, a quick guide to URLs follows:

- Google—https://www.google.com/goodtoknow/online-safety/ security-tools/
- Microsoft—https://www.microsoft.com/security/online-privacy/ overview.aspx
- Yahoo—http://security.yahoo.com/
- LinkedIn—https://www.linkedin.com/settings/
- Facebook—https://www.facebook.com/settings/?tab=privacy&privacy_ source=settings_menu
- MySpace—https://www.myspace.com/my/settings/account/privacy
- LiveJournal—https://www.livejournal.com/manage/settings/?cat=privacy
- Twitter—https://twitter.com/settings/account

Odds are that you don't want to make yourself completely invisible, even though most of these tools allow that. However, if there is a specific site that represents you in a less than positive light, you may wish to hide that one.

Since Facebook and Twitter are common sources of one's poor choices being made obvious to others, there is a tool that allows you to scrub these profiles specifically. SimpleWash (simplewa.sh) will scan your posts and alert you to any that you may wish to delete or alter. Like all such scanning tools, you shouldn't completely rely on its accuracy, but it's a good check to make sure that you caught everything.

LOADING SOCIAL MEDIA

At this point, you should have a good idea what interests the people with whom you wish to work. If you've been following the process in this book, you already have a blog. If you don't, create one at Google or WordPress under your real name. That will make it nicely searchable. Then, write three to five blog posts, each targeting an issue that you wish to have come up during the interview. Be sure to proof each post before you hit "submit," as once it's up, it's out there and will be cached in numerous search engines. If you wish, you can back date some posts to make it look like you've been an expert longer than you truly have. If you do this, though, be sure to do it at the time of creation; otherwise, search engines may show that you've adjusted the dates to make yourself seem more of an expert. If you think there's a chance that you'll be caught, and you're applying to an organization that is particularly touchy about such things (government and military), it's best not to try that technique.

You can do also manage your profile at microblogging sites like Twitter. Find others in your field and start replying to their posts—but only if you can add to the discussion. A good metric that employers use when looking at people on Twitter is the broadcast-to-discussion ratio. There should be at least the same number of discussion posts as there are initial posts. Hopefully, you'll get some good discussions going and the ratio will be much higher than this.

As you create and communicate on social media, you'll become more aware of the issues you are discussing. If you choose issues that interest your targets, you'll become more aware of what drives them. This will help you to be more interesting in the interview but also will make you look better in their preliminary checks against you. Most importantly, it allows you to refer interviewers towards something that drives them towards you. If they haven't checked you out, try to lead the discussion towards something you blogged about. Then, in your follow-up letter, you can refer to your blog and try to increase their interest in you.

CUSTOM RÉSUMÉ

If you've created your master résumé as described earlier in this book, now is the time to adjust it for the position you're currently pursuing. First, run through it and remove anything that doesn't help you tell a story that would be interesting to your targets. With luck, this will get you down to one or two pages. If not, run through it again and mark the items based on how objectively interesting you consider them. Put a number at the front of each line, marking each story from 1 (somewhat interesting) to 4 (extremely interesting). Pull out all number ones and see if that gets you down to a good size. If not, purge all the twos, and so on.

When the résumé is at a reasonable size, go through it line by line and adjust the content to reflect the language you expect your targets to respond to. You've mapped your metaphors and know the language they are likely to use, so spend a bit of time with thesaurus.com and see what improvements you can make. Once the résumé is fully adjusted, look at the fonts and colors on your target's website. You don't necessarily want a perfect match, but you want something in the same font family and a similar color scheme. Consider viewing the HTML source code of their webpage and seeing what font is listed. Run their logo through the font detector at www.myfonts.com/WhatTheFont/ and pick a similar (but not identical) one for your résumé headers.

For colors, read their website source or use an online color scheme tool like www.colorcombos.com/grabcolors.html. This will give you a starting point for a color scheme to use for the custom deliverables discussed later. For your résumé, find a light color used on the website and see if you can find paper of a similar hue for printing on. Then, if you wish to avoid your résumé looking like a rip-off, pick the dominant colors and simplify the color hex code. For example, consider a website whose dominant colors are the following:

- Green—00a681
- Blue—00558a
- Light grey—dae3e8
- Dark grey—656565
- Orange—e07400

You could pick a light grey paper and use the following colors for text:

- Green—00aa88
- Blue—005588
- Dark grey—666666
- Orange—ee7700

This simplification technique doesn't always work, so if these colors look jarring when compared to the original, go back to the originals for your basic set. If you want to try an advanced approach, you can use tools like Color Schemer (www.colorschemer.com/online.html) or Color Scheme Designer (colorschemedesigner.com) to come up with complementary colors. However, for this example, the simpler version will suffice.

You wouldn't have to use them all, but you could choose the green for your major headers, a blue for your date/company subheaders, and put a dark grey border around the page. This will be pleasing to the eye and should particularly please your interviewers, as it will be a set of colors that they see every day, and you'll seem like a more comfortable and safer choice.

If you do not own a color printer, you can always go to an office store and have them do your printing for you.

CUSTOM COVER LETTER

The cover letter process will be much like that of the résumé. You have your fonts and colors; make them match. Then choose a nice large font size for the letter (12 pt or 14 pt) and a larger size for the letter header. Keep the letter very simple. Explain what you think you'd be able to do for your target company, and inform them that you'll be calling to request an interview. The point of the letter is not to lay everything on the line; it's to make them more likely to respond favorably to your request for an interview. That's all. If you try to explain too much, you risk causing confusion, and that will work against you.

While there are many ways to style the cover letter, a three-paragraph approach often works very well. See Figure 9.1 for an example. In the first paragraph, introduce yourself. Explain the skills you have, some successes you've made for other companies, and, in general, why you're awesome. The second paragraph should explain why you think their organization is awesome and that you'd like to help them become even more awesome. Then, in the third paragraph, state that you'd like to have a further discussion and that you will be calling at three specific times. Ask that, if any of those times will not work, they let you know what times would be better.

Next, you should sign the letter, attach your résumé, and send it. Wait about four days, then send an email version of the same. Finally, at each of the scheduled times when you said you'd call, do so, and be prepared to leave a message that states who you are and the reason you are calling; reference the letter(s) you sent and say when you'll call again. See Figure 9.2 for an example. At the end of the three calls, send a follow-up email stating your regret that you were not able to reach them, reiterate why you want to talk to them, and leave your contact info.

Adriaan Roosen   April 1, 2014
Executive Vice President

Elsevier
360 Park Ave S
New York, NY 10010

Mr. Roosen,

Thank you for taking the time to read this note. I believe that we might be able to help one another. I have 13 years of experience in information technology, with a focus on system failure and continual improvement. I have managed incidents and served as a team leader, and believe that I am ready to do more. After taking down crime rings, preventing intrusions, and helping my organizations improve, I find that I have helped them change as much as they are willing to. I believe that I could greatly help your organization.

After researching all of the important firms in the publishing industry, I have settled on Elsevier as the most relevant. Your acquisition history shows clear vision and your rate of growth, while promising, suggests that you may be experiencing some of the challenges that I enjoy addressing. If you are finding that your support volume has grown beyond your ability to cope effectively, that Elsevier's larger size makes it a greater target, or that projects are facing ever-increasing delays, I think I can help.

Since I wish to help make the publishing industry a better place and your firm is the best in the industry, I thought I'd just save everyone a lot of time and see if you'd be willing to meet with me and explore whether we'd be able to work together. I think that, by working together, we could build something much better than either of us could accomplish on our own. I will be calling you at 9:00 AM on Monday the 7th, at 1:00 PM on Wednesday the 9th, and again at 4:00 PM on Friday the 11th. If you are busy during these times, please let me know what time works best for you. I hope our mutual schedules allow us to talk soon.

Sincerely,

Jennifer Quantum
Jennifer Quantum

Figure 9.1 Example Cover Letter

Voicemail Script: Initial Call - April 7th, 9:00 AM

Hello Mister Roosen. This is Jennifer Quantum calling on April 7th at 9:00 AM, as promised. I am sorry that I was unable to reach you, but I look forward to talking to you on Wednesday. As per my email, if these times do not work well with your schedule, please let me know. I can be reached via email at jenny2@authority.com or via phone at 555-867-5309. As mentioned in my email, I would like have a short discussion with you as to whether I can help you with some of your current business challenges. I believe it would be a good use of both your time and mine.

Again, while I will be contacting you twice more, if you wish to reach me, please call me back at 555-867-5309.

Thank you.

Figure 9.2 Example Voicemail Script

This approach shows that you have initiative, drive, and follow-through. Even if you do not succeed in reaching anyone, you've planted a seed that can be used as you follow the same approach with others in the same organization. Work your way through the prospective interviewer list. Supposing you have identified five people in your target organization; if at the end of the process, you've sent five letters and ten emails and made 15 phone calls over the course of many days, you can assume they're not interested. This is when you can make your last-ditch contact attempt before moving on.

To do this, identify the target organization's largest competitor and simply write an email to each of your interview contacts. In the email, thank them for their time, express sadness that you were unable to connect with them, and say that things are looking promising with another company. Then mention the competitor by name, and let the target organization decide whether or not to contact you.

This approach is not without risk, as the organization may know someone at that firm and be in a position to check up on you; but all you have to do is send one letter to the competing organization to be on the right side of truth. After all, if you've managed to go through the process without getting a contact, you might as well reach out to their competitors. You've done the industry research already and now need to investigate the next potential interview board.

TARGETED NETWORKING

One thing you can do to push the envelope is attend physical networking events. You should do this if you've uncovered affiliations with specific organizations. This may be a target who attends a monthly technical user group. It may be an executive who is active in a service group like Rotary International or Kiwanis. It may be a salesperson active in a lead-trading group like BNI. All of these groups are fairly open to new and guest members. However, if you plan to go, make sure you support the core purpose of the group and/or are interested in the topic being discussed.

True networking can take years, so as you go through this process, remember that you're not just looking for your next job, you're working toward the job after that. Learn what the people you're talking to need and try to find a way to help them. If, over time, you help a lot of people, you've built up a large pile of intangible credits that you can cash in when you need some help yourself. Don't expect a job to come out of this process. It's nice if that happens, but it is not guaranteed.

With that in mind, before you go prepare a few folders with a generic cover letter, résumé, and business card. If you're running low on business cards, order a new batch, as you don't want to run out. Have all of your folders easily at hand and be prepared to hand one to your target if the occasion arises. It's a matter of being prepared. Try to have a discussion about the group or topic and see if you can lead him or her to discussing business needs. If he or she has a resource problem, mention that you're in the market and hand him or her the folder. Then, in your follow-up email, mention the networking event as well as the basic information in the cover letter.

It should be stressed that to succeed in this approach, you must be comfortable with subtle social interactions. If that is difficult for you, you should probably avoid attending networking groups only for the purpose of getting a job. Attend if you're interested in the topic, by all means, but don't expect to be able to schmooze a stranger into giving you an interview. A failure here could destroy your chances, so it's a poor risk to take unless you know you can carry it off. If you find yourself being consistently interested in the topics, and you become known, it will get easier over time to leverage those relationships.

CHAPTER *10*

The Phone Interview: Dial M for Meeting

Phone interviews can come about in many ways, but in the end, either you call them or they call you. If they call you, and you're lucky, it will be someone you've already researched. If not, schedule it a few days out if possible so you can do some preliminary research. Aside from that, the goal of scheduling the phone interview is to identify a particular time at which you will be available to have a good discussion.

If the interviewer asks if you have time right now to chat, the answer is a polite "no." Doing so gives all the power to the interviewer and gives you almost no benefit whatsoever. Explain that you have another appointment in a few minutes and find out what other times your interviewer may be available. That allows you time to prepare.

Even if you have done your research already, set aside enough lead time to do some backfill research before you have the actual discussion.

PREREQUISITES FOR A GOOD DISCUSSION

It should be fairly obvious, but be sure to schedule this discussion at a time when you can reliably be somewhere quiet, with good reception, no distractions, and easy access to your resources. You'll want to be able to refer to your quick reference sheets during the discussion. You *may* need to be able to do quick searches on the Internet, but that can be risky, as the Internet can be quite distracting.

Once you've picked your time and place with the person scheduling the interview, spend a bit of time trying to determine any interview specifics so you can be prepared. This can be as easy as just asking if there's anything you should prepare for the interview. Odds are that they'll tell you "nothing," which is just an indicator to dig a bit deeper. What you're looking for is confirmation that your assumptions about the organization (culture, approach to work, style of management, etc.) are correct. Ask the names of the people you'll be speaking with.

Ask what their titles are. Then ask if there is a specific problem they're expecting to solve with the new position. Finally, ask for their email addresses so you can send an updated version of your résumé prior to the phone interview.

Any responses to these questions will be useful. Review the list of names against your list of probable interviewers. Anyone new should be researched prior to the interview. This information should be used to tweak the résumé to match their likely metaphors so you can send the updated résumé. This helps establish your credibility as someone who follows through and also lays some groundwork for success. If you get metaphorical conflict, where hobbies and generation collide, fall back to industry or organization metaphors.

GOALS FOR THE PHONE INTERVIEW

Chatting on the phone is not the same as an interview. An interview has goals. On the side of the interviewer, his or her goal is to identify whether or not it is worth his or her time to talk further with you. If his or her current pain level is high, he or she will be motivated to bring you in. If it is low, he or she will be looking for ways to kick you off the list of candidates. Most people who do this initial round are not the ones who feel the pain, so go into the interview presuming you are at a disadvantage.

Your goals are twofold. Your primary goal is to get a real interview. Your secondary goal is to get information to help you succeed in that real interview. That's it. Keep focused on these two items and avoid any tendency to chat informally. Answer their questions and ask questions of your own, with each minute spent on the phone aimed at helping you advance towards these two goals.

THE ACTUAL PHONE INTERVIEW

When the actual phone interview starts, you should be in a quiet room with a reliable phone. You should have a pad of paper for notes and a small stack of notes that list your target's specific information. It's tempting to do it with a laptop or tablet, but the click of keys can be quite distracting and technology can fail you. Stick with older, more reliable, and silent technologies. You can always transcribe your handwritten notes into your preferred system after the interview. It is often best to hold these interviews in your kitchen. Obviously, do not do this while cooking or if the kitchen is a public area prone to disruption. If you can clear the room for the duration of your call, you can lay your papers out in a row along a counter and hold the interview standing up. When people stand and speak, their voices naturally sound more forceful and resonate more deeply. The lessons learned by professional singers also work well for phone interviews. Stand, breathe, and know what you're going to say before you say it. While it is true that dead air during an interview sounds bad, stumbling over your words and reversing what you've said sounds a whole lot worse.

As you talk, try to face a reflective surface—bring in a mirror if you have to—and watch your body language. This will help keep you from slouching, folding your arms, or adopting any posture that can affect your voice. Smiling makes your voice sound friendlier. All of this will also help make the experience more genuine for yourself and for the person you're talking to.

As the phone interview continues, you should be able to determine whether or not you are progressing towards your primary goal. Once you've answered their questions sufficiently to be confident that they're not going to weed you out, it's time for you to start asking questions of your own. This includes knowing whether you are going to fit into the company, looking at the corporate culture, and identifying whether you'd be able to work for your potential new boss.

Questions to ask involve the basic theme "What is it like to work at Organization X?" Open questions may be hard for your interviewers to answer, so ask more specific questions, like these:

- What is the average number of hours worked per week? If I work more than the average, how would it reflect on me?
- What percentage of the work week is expected to be used solving problems or creating value versus planning work?
- It takes time to get up to speed on anything. If I am selected for this job, how long do you expect it to take me to reach peak efficiency?
- Do you have any expectations for the sort of work I would be doing in 30, 60, or 90 days?

These questions probe for how much you're expected to work and how fast you're expected to get things done without making it sound as if you're lazy. If you suspect that what they're looking for will be difficult to find, too expensive for them, or flat-out impossible, this is your chance to start changing their expectations. Ideally, you would adjust their expectations to be more realistic while also making it evident that you are the right person for the job as they now see it.

PLANNING THE IN-PERSON INTERVIEW

Once things look promising enough to lead towards an in-person interview, you must take advantage of the opportunity to actually talk to people. You should have their quick reference sheets sitting in front of you, with details as to which metaphors you think they'll respond. As you talk to them on the phone, try to make references to what you think will resonate. Score each metaphor you use according to a scale like the following:

Failed   Worked Great

A simple six-item system works well here, where a 1 indicates failure and a 6 indicates wild success. The 2 through 5 give you a bit of room to work with, while the absence of a middle number helps you avoid the trap of scoring every attempt in the middle of the range.

As the phone interview winds to a close, you should plan the physical interview. Pick a day, not a time, when you can be free. Within that day, try to choose a morning time to start the interview, but not first thing in the morning. In organizations that work from 8 AM to 5 PM, anytime between 9 and 10 AM is a good starting time. This gives you time to get lost on the way to the building and gives your interviewers time to deal with any issues that arose overnight so they can focus on talking with you.

Again, identify the specific people who will be interviewing you so you can update your research ahead of time. Then, schedule it sufficiently far out that you have a chance to do another round of backfill on the research and, if you choose, customize your portfolio for the opportunity.

CHAPTER 11

The Portfolio: Items to Leave Behind

One of the keys to standing out from other candidates is to have a portfolio you can leave behind at an interview. Physical portfolios are quite rare in most fields these days, so anyone who takes the effort to create one automatically appears better than everyone else.

THE PORTFOLIO PROCESS

One approach that works well is to use plain two-pocket folders. It is growing more difficult to find plain folders, but an office supply store should have at least a few options. You can also check online, but try to find folders that are professional and not emblazoned with the logos of other firms. Plain black is generally a good choice, but well-stocked stores may have other color options. Avoid lighter colors, as they show staining, and avoid gloss finishes, as they show scratches.

One side of the folder should be filled with documents about you. At a minimum, this should be your cover letter and résumé. However, if you have done public work, such as a flyer or paper that you think is particularly good, you can include such items on that side of the folder as well. The other side is for the company you are targeting. This will be reserved for customized documentation, such as market research or brainstorming of ideas to help the business.

Some folders have a little inset in them for a business card. If this slot is available, you should use it. When you leave your portfolio behind, your targets will be reminded of you every time they look at it.

You may also wish to have a separate folder in a different color for sensitive documents that you will not be leaving behind.

CUSTOM DOCUMENTS

A critical piece of this process is to have custom documents to leave behind. The nature of these documents will vary from target to target, but in general their purpose is to indicate to your target organization that you have taken the time to consider its needs. Such documents can consider business challenges, such as a desire to push into new markets, ways to improve internal efficiency, or ways to better service existing customers. These documents should be highly visual, as interviewers are not going to read them during the interview and will be unlikely to read large blocks of text after the interview.

One common reason that organizations create new positions is to branch out into a new market. Thus, documents that reflect market research can be quite valuable. One way to approach this is to look for holes in the competitive landscape. Most organizations have competitors, and these competitors can be easily found through a few searches. Look for independent analysis of the industry that you are targeting. Turn off your Internet ad blocker and do searches on each of your target organization's products and services. Build a list of competitors and rank them based on how well-known they seem to be in the market. Then, review each competitor's site and build a list of features. Work to move the list of features into a single one-page document and make a comparison table. This table should list competitors across the top and features down the side, with a checkmark in each box that indicates if that feature is present. Then, place a dash in each box where that feature is lacking.

This chart should make it easy to identify which competitors are missing features and which are well-positioned. You should only list features that have value in the market. Many products suffer from feature bloat that makes them appear more important than they truly are. You should avoid listing any of your target organization's products or services. Those are well-known by the organization, and anything you get wrong will be pointed out and counted against you. It doesn't matter if the source of the poor information is their website—you will be viewed as the one who guessed wrong, so it's safer to just leave your target organization out completely.

Once this document is generated, you should apply a reasonable font and colors to it, as discussed in the Repositioning chapter.

Flow-based documents can also be useful. If you are applying for a support role, include a document that indicates how problems are reported and handled. If you are hoping to help create a new market, create a document that shows how sales will work within that market. If you want to create a new technology, make a flow diagram that shows how that technology will work. This way, when you discuss your hopes and dreams, you can pull out the document and walk through the flow as you explain your ideas to your interviewers.

Other documents can include different ways to bundle products or services (block diagrams), ways to define new markets (demographic diagrams), and timelines for industry changes.

This can seem overwhelming, but such work is easily done with free tools like Inkscape (inkscape.org), LibreOffice (www.libreoffice.org), and Gimp (www.gimp.org). These free replacements for applications like Adobe Illustrator, Microsoft Office, and Adobe Photoshop have learning curves, but there are many tutorials and instructional videos online. Start by sketching your idea on paper, then work it into a digital format. Then, throw that away and rework it into a better version that includes the organization's colors and fonts.

If you are not used to a creative process like this, doing a throwaway draft may seem counterintuitive, but it often results in a much better version of the idea. You usually don't get nearly as much improvement on subsequent iterations, so focus on the second version of your idea, then move on. It may help to take your first idea to a friend or two and get their opinions on where it's unclear. This will help form your concept for the final version.

Finally, in at least one final document, introduce a small typo. This is so when you use the document in the interview, you can notice the typo, circle it with a pen and, in the second interview, provide a version of the document with that error corrected. Ideally, you would also adjust the document based on feedback you received in the interview, but while you have no control over what others will say, by introducing a deliberate error you still get to show improvement. To prevent people from thinking that you just didn't proofread your materials, try to make the introduced error appear reasonable. Think of typos that are still properly spelled words ("it" for "is") or places where a small word like "a" is left out.

Aim for at least two such custom documents in your first interview, then add one document for each subsequent interview you have, updating each document as you learn more about what the organization needs.

BUSINESS CARDS

Everyone wants an awesome business card, but face it—with all the work that must be done to get a solid customized résumé, a good cover letter, and some custom documents, the business card is going to get shorted. To create a card that is good enough, get some inspiration by looking at other people's cards, then try your hand at a design. Google Image search is a great place to start. Just search on "best business cards" or "business card template" and look at what others have done. There will be some with special shapes, embossing, or fancy multi-layer printing. Ignore those, as they will not be very cost-effective. Also ignore those that have a lot of complex layout. Instead, look at how color is used and the overall design.

At the bare minimum, a business card should contain your name and an email address. A catchy title, phone number, and other such information can be useful, but the more you veer from "normal," the riskier it gets. Remember, the goal is not to show off how awesome you are at designing business cards, unless you are hoping to get a job doing just that.

While you can always use your current title (if employed), consider giving yourself a clever title like "Employee of the Month: January–December (next year)" or "Looking for a Boss." Since your card should never be seen by anyone at your current place of work, there's little risk to this practice, and a memorable title can be invaluable in the job search process. Add your own hobbies to your card to make you seem more well-rounded. If you can strike the right balance and give interesting and useful information on the card without adding anything too frivolous, you can create very strong connections in the brains of the people you talk to. The stronger these connections, the less likely they are to forget you, and the more likely it will be that they'll contact you when they need something.

Once designed, use one of the tools listed earlier (Inkscape, Gimp, LibreOffice, or Microsoft Word) to generate a basic sheet of business cards with cut lines. Save the document as a PDF and take it to a printing store or office supply store with a print department. Explain that you need a small number of cards printed on heavy stock and that you need them cut. It shouldn't cost very much to do a small run. While they won't be as good as professionally designed and printed business cards, they'll be unique to you, and that will help to set you apart from the rest of the pack.

Finally, avoid the "print your business card for free" services. They often print their name on the back of your card and use lower-quality materials, which does nothing but spread confusion and make you look cheap. An office store can print a set of 100 decent business cards starting at $20. This is more than sufficient so long as you're careful to only hand cards out to people who can help you get a job.

NOTES ON DESIGN

It is unreasonable to expect to become a great designer in the limited time you have, and it is better spent on research and preparation for your interview. Your goal is to be good enough to look better than those who didn't put in any work at all. With that in mind, there are a few design rules of thumb to keep in mind for the business cards as well as the custom documents that you will be generating for the portfolio

Fonts, Colors, and Gradients

Using the same technique you used for the Cover Letter section, verify the color scheme and fonts that you will be using for the more advanced documents. You may need a few more colors to use on these documents, so if your target is relatively monochrome, use the color tools mentioned earlier to find other colors that look good with the basic schemes.

One useful trick is to take advantage of gradient support in vector tools. When you have a color scheme, you can select gradients that fade from one color to another. If you keep with the standard of having black text on a white background, you can also fade any color to black or white. This must be done carefully to avoid looking amateurish, but when done consistently and minimally, it can add a great sense of depth to your images. Do not do this with text. It takes a lot of experience to get gradients to work with text, and often involves special adjustments to outline and shadow objects. If you are not a graphic designer, it is best to just let text be text.

Minimalism

Clutter is the enemy. Avoid it at all costs. Remember that you have both the front and back of each document to work with, though just working with the front is much easier. After you make the initial design, run it past your friends and ask if it looks too cluttered. If so, simplify where you can. The purpose of a business card is to allow people to contact you. The purpose of a business document is to convey a single idea and allow people to explore it. All other uses, such as making you look particularly creative or risky, are ancillary. If you have the technical and creative chops to pull something like that off, you'll know. If you're not certain, embrace minimalism.

Visual Metaphors

As you've done your research on your interviewers, you should have a guess as to what metaphors they use to think about things. If one of them is an avid golfer, for example, you can use language around "getting a hole in one" or "avoiding hazards." You can back this up in your custom documents with images involving golf clubs, courses, or balls. Similar visual metaphors can be used for hobbies like knitting or reading, or causes as indicated by membership in groups focusing on poverty or conservation.

Keep your design simple and visually clean. Remember that metaphors serve as frameworks, so a little bit goes a long way. If you're targeting someone who is interested in golf, they will respond well to a document that has a single golf club in one area, a green as a background, and a hole somewhere else. They will likely not respond any better, and possibly respond poorly, to a document that uses an entire golf course as the metaphor with tees, greens, and hazards all over the document.

Think first about graphics that will support both your text and the metaphor that you are using. Remember that you can use them as both primary and supporting objects. For example, a document with a single graphic featured prominently will attract the target's interest, but the subtle use of graphics, such as for bullets and horizontal dividers, will support your metaphor in a more subtle way.

Many images can be found through basic image searches, though you will not want to use them directly. The Google search "item filetype:svg" will help you find vector graphics that can be imported directly into Inkscape. Once there, you can adjust the colors and lines to match your document's style. It is wise to check the license of such works before you use them, but for any image, be it a directly editable .svg file or a bitmapped .png or .jpg, you can always trace over parts of it in a tool like Inkscape or use it for inspiration and create your own work that is similar, but not identical, to the original source.

This makes it easy to illustrate your documents in ways that will make your portfolio stand out from any other "walls of text" documents.

Copyeditors

Odds are that you can't edit your own work. As you build your portfolio, you will have created a résumé, a cover letter, and at least two custom documents. You may have anonymized versions of public documents you've created. You may have blog articles that you've turned into articles or internal reports that you've scrubbed for public sharing.

It can be very useful to get a second pair of eyes to look over what you've done. Copyeditors are easy to find. Do a search on "copyeditor for hire," place ads on sites like Craigslist, or hire one off of the CE-L copyeditor freelancers list (www.copyediting-l.info). Professional copyeditors will often charge between $100 and $300 to review a smallish set of documents—and they are well worth the investment. Most of this book advocates using free tools and services where possible, but in this one case, you very much get what you pay for. Pay for it.

Print Shops

To be successful in this endeavor, you will have to print out your work. It is tempting to save money by doing this at home, but the difference in quality between heavy semi gloss paper stock run through a high-resolution printer and normal paper printed on your home inkjet printer is huge. Small runs are fairly inexpensive and can often be done at any office store. Find the person behind the desk and explain what you're doing. You'll want one type of paper stock for your résumé and cover letter and another for your custom documents. The clerk should be able to assist you. If they cannot, find a better print shop.

If you have enough of an understanding of how print shops work that you know what specific paper stock (weight, color, and finish) you want and know how you want it printed, you can often do this process online and just show up at the print shop to pick up the end result. If there's an error, you may have to wait while they rerun the job, but most print shops are understanding about such things.

A full run of a reasonably complete portfolio can cost between $30 and $70, which is an entirely reasonable investment, especially if it gets you the job.

CHAPTER *12*

Thinking about Money: Making the Most of Change

No matter where you are in the process, it is useful to think about salary negotiation. However, it is wise to be prepared. The technique discussed in this chapter is only one way to do it. There are as many others as there are books on job hunting and negotiation. The view taken here is that any job you land through this process will have a much higher chance of job satisfaction than where you are today, so any money above what your current or last job had is an improvement.

Everyone wants their next job to be the one that makes them rich, but each employer wants each new employee to be one that makes them more profitable. Since employers set the salaries, they often win. This approach to total compensation can help even the odds, but always keep in mind that your real goal is a win/win situation in which both you and your new employer wind up better off for hiring you.

TOTAL COMPENSATION

The core idea behind total compensation is to capture everything your current or most recent employer gives you. This means capturing not only what you are given in salary, but also converting nonmonetary items like benefits, software, and hardware to hard dollars. This is best done with a spreadsheet.

Calculate your annual pretax salary; that's the first line. To this, add calculations (by year) for nonmonetary compensation, like these examples:

- Bonuses (end of year, profit sharing, project-based, commissions, quarterly MBOs)
- Education (training classes, conferences)
- Travel and lodging for education opportunities
- Any monies paid to help sustain certifications and professional memberships

- Insurance paid by company (health, dental, vision)
- Retirement paid by company (401(k) match, IRA match, management fees)
- Vacation and sick days, flexible time, volunteer time
- Reimbursements (cell phones, mobile Internet devices)
- Tools (computers as factored into a yearly cost, software subscriptions)

Add these together to obtain your total annual compensation. Then, if you're considering a job in a new place, factor in a multiplier for cost of living increase (or decrease). Be sure to support this number with statistics in case you're called on it. Searches on "cost of living" for where you are and where you'd be moving help, and do searches on sites like bankrate.com and payscale.com. If you're physically relocating to a larger metro area, this one step could make the difference between being able to live comfortably while working at the job of your dreams and being unable to support yourself financially, no matter how otherwise rewarding the job might be – so do your research.

The final number will give you an answer to the question of "What are you making now?" Armed with that, you can reply with a higher number than your base salary, but one that is defensible if you are challenged.

Finally, make a new column on the spreadsheet and fill in specific areas you'd like to improve. Some people are motivated by hardware and need to boost their annual computer budget to be happy. Some want more educational opportunities. Unsurprisingly, most want a higher take-home salary. Add all these together, and add 10% to the top and bottom of that number, and you have your asking range. Be willing to be flexible within the total compensation calculation; if a lower salary is offered, you might ask for a higher education budget. So long as the total compensation offered is higher than where you are today, and each relevant individual line item is higher, you're moving forward. You can always renegotiate later—though if this process is successful, you'll be spending so much time doing work you enjoy that you may not bother.

If you've been unemployed for a while, your baseline may be what you need to live on and will not necessarily be linked to your previous job. Pick an asking range that is 10% above and below the average for that job as reported on various salary surveys. Make sure the bottom end of your range is not below your actual financial minimum.

Direct Compensation	Amount	Adj.	Total
Base salary	$50,000.00	1	$50,000.00
Commission bonus	$5,000.00	1	$5,000.00
Education support			
Annual conference: plane ticket	$500.00	1	$500.00
Annual conference: hotel, 2 nights @ $200/night	$200.00	2	$400.00
Annual conference: food, 3 days @ $75/day	$75.00	3	$225.00
Biennial training: plane ticket	$500.00	0.5	$250.00
Biennial training: hotel, 5 nights @ $200/night	$200.00	2.5	$500.00
Biennial training: food, 5 days @ $75/day	$75.00	2.5	$187.50
Biennial training: tuition	$2,500.00	0.5	$1,250.00
Certification and membership support			
User group dues	$25.00	1	$25.00
Certification maintenance	$75.00	1	$75.00
Insurance			
Health*	$1,500.00	1	$1,500.00
Dental*	$200.00	1	$200.00
401(k) (match up to 3%)	$1,000.00	1	$1,000.00
Vacation			
Two weeks' paid vacation each year	$961.54	2	$1,923.08
Tools			
Laptop (every two years)	$2,000.00	0.5	$1,000.00
Windows Enterprise/Ultimate license (every four years)[†]	$265.00	0.25	$66.25
Office Pro license (every four years)[†]	$400.00	0.25	$100.00
Cost of living adjustment[‡]			15.00%
Total			
Current			$64,201.83
Current + cost of living adjustment			$73,832.10
*Estimated			
[†]From Amazon.com			
[‡]From bankrate.com			

In this example, notice that even though the base salary is $50,000, the current total compensation comes to $64,201.83. This is because of the contributions to insurance, vacation, and training, plus the commission. Additionally, there is a cost of living difference of 15% between where the job currently is and where the new job target is. This brings the total compensation estimate to $73,832.10. Since negotiation works better with ranges, the $+/-10\%$ rule would bring the asking range to $66,448.89 to $81,215.31 or, to keep things simple, $67k–$81k.

This is, of course, an annual salary calculation. If you wished to have a discussion around hourly rates, just divide the total number of working hours in a year. Assuming two weeks of vacation, that's 50 weeks at 40 hours per week. Thus, in this example, you could expect an hourly rate of $33.22 to $40.61.

CHAPTER 13

Before the Interview: Plan to Succeed

To a certain extent, the entire book up until this point has been about the preinterview process. There are also some things that should be done after the interview is scheduled but before it takes place. This mostly involves logistics, but there is also a bit of analytics and practice involved. Fundamentally, the first time you do anything, it's going to be of less-than-ideal quality. Often, it'll just be flat-out bad. The best way to improve is to make mistakes—but you don't want to do that in actual interviews, so you need to prepare.

PHYSICAL INVESTIGATION

If you live in the same metro area in which the job is, go there. The easiest way to be late is to get lost. If you're driving, know where you're going. If you're taking public transportation, know the route. Take a trip there during the same time of day you'd travel on the real day. This gives you a reasonable feel for the traffic and helps you check your route. If you're interviewing on a weekday, make sure to test your drive under those conditions. If you make the run on Saturday but the interview is on Thursday, there will almost certainly be traffic differences.

If you do not live there, verify the map on several online mapping services, such as Google Maps, MapQuest, and Bing Maps. Once you know the route, pull up Google Street View and make sure you can identify the landmarks. Drive the route mentally, to minimize surprises.

If you can get there, or have access to good photos, look at the cars in the parking lot. Read the bumper stickers and take note of the quality of the cars. Bumper stickers can disclose information about hobbies, causes, and political affiliations. Vanity and special license plates can give you similar information. Linking specific cars to your interviewers may be difficult. After all, you can't just use a police database to run a plate search. However, this data can be an indicator that, when combined with other information you've uncovered about people who work for the business, can be a good way to identify aspects of the culture that may not be apparent from online resources alone.

Car quality can give you a feel for how well the employees are paid. As with everything else, this is just an indicator, not a certainty—and more than other indicators, this one can be quite misleading. The biggest thing to check is whether there are reserved spots for managers and if those spots have noticeably better vehicles than other spots. Such a disparity can indicate not only a financial difference but, more importantly, a social difference in how management treats employees.

While you are physically there, you have some options to consider. These may not always be wise but are worth considering. Entering the building can give you data about how people interact with one another and the dress code but can cause you to be challenged in ways you'd not prefer. Peering in windows and digging through trash could get you in serious trouble and might be illegal. The safest option is to just drive through the parking lot, then leave. Another option is available if there is a public area near the office. Locations like coffeehouses and parks allow you to linger within sight of the main door so you can note the types of clothing people wear, the traffic patterns as they go in and out the door, the general level of friendliness, and so on. This may not give you hard data, but it helps with your overall impression of the organization.

QUESTION PLANNING

Remember, the entire process for getting the job surrounds taking control of the eventual interview. This is where you finally get your chance. Interviews have common questions. The entire premise of this book is that you're not going to get a great job by answering the questions with a standard "right" answer. Simply making the interviewer like you isn't enough. That's the game everyone is playing. After all, your competition has the same interview books you do and has practiced the same standard questions, so if you practice, you are, at best, no worse off than they are. You are, however, no better off, either. And if you don't practice, you run the risk of interviewing poorly, even if you've done all the other preparation—so you've got to do it.

This is not a book that will tell you how to answer questions like "What is your greatest weakness?" or "Why do you want to work here?"

or "Where do you see yourself in ten years?" There are tons of books for that already, and the world does not need another. Pick up one of those, but pick it up in audio format. It doesn't matter if it's a CD, MP3, or video. The important thing is that someone asks you the question and you pause playback to answer. If you are currently commuting, you can practice this in the car. Otherwise, try it out at home. Run through each of the questions repeatedly until you have a good answer for each—one that feels natural but does not sound scripted. For most people, this will take three to five times through the list of questions.

As you work through the possible answers to each question, consider whether you can reference one of your résumé stories. Consider how others would answer the question and see if you can come up with a more creative and memorable answer. You know some of the questions you're going to be asked, so prepare in a way that will make you stand out but also supports the rest of your message.

If you do not have the budget to use one of the other resources, visit your library, check out your local unemployment office, look around online, or have a friend read you the list of questions found in Appendix B of this book. Additionally, this list of questions will be available as a free audio download.

Dangerous Questions

If you anticipate dangerous questions arising in the course of the interview, consider how you'll respond to them. Such questions can involve gaps in your employment history, a history of job hopping, situations in which you've been fired or quit in anger, or anything else that might raise alarms from things they see in your résumé or online.

In almost all cases, the appropriate response is to acknowledge their concerns, admit to any issues you may have had, and explain what you learned in addressing them. As you practice your questions, keep this in mind, and add questions of this type to the list.

Remember that the truth has many facets. Perhaps you were let go for what you believe to be prejudiced reasons. Raising that concern in an interview is not likely to endear you to the interviewer, so find a tactful way to state things. There's a reason that bands break up over "artistic differences" and politicians resign to "spend more time with their family."

TIME PLANNING

Interviewers like to set aside either one hour for an interview or about thirty minutes for each person conducting the interview. Thus, expect to receive interview requests scheduled for one to two hours. However, most interviewers do not expect to be presented with a prepared interviewee who has a portfolio and a set of ideas for improvement. This will take them by surprise and can often cause the interview itself to stretch out significantly. It is not uncommon for a morning interview to turn into a lunch interview and then extend into the afternoon.

Because of this tendency, it is best to block off the entire day on your schedule for the interview. If it ends when scheduled, you'll have time to relax and get other things done. If it extends, you won't have to worry about rescheduling anything. At the end of the interview, thank everyone, and just walk out the door, leaving behind the customized portfolios that you designed for the job.

Arrival can be a bit different. Plan to arrive at least half an hour early. This will give you time to find a parking place (if you're driving), check yourself to remove any lint or cat hair, do a quick breath freshener, and prepare to go in. Arrive ten minutes early for the interview and be prepared wait in the entryway until your interviewer is ready. If there is a receptionist present, introduce yourself and ask them to notify your interviewer. If company material is available, read that. This will cause you to appear interested in the business. If such material is not available, review your résumé and portfolio.

If you are physically able, stand while you wait. This way, when your interviewer arrives, they see someone with energy at a similar level as them. When you are sitting, you appear at disadvantage, with the other person being physically above you. You don't want to dominate your interviewers, so if you're excessively tall, you may choose to sit. But you don't want to unnecessarily place yourself at a disadvantage.

APPEARANCE

It can help to engage in "mirroring" to help build rapport. You can learn more about this concept from various social engineering and psychology books. In general, the concept is to assume similar postures and physical actions as your interviewer. This makes the person you are mirroring feel more rapport with you and, over time, feel like they and you are similar enough to grow the relationship. Try not to be identical, as that can be creepy; but if you dress somewhat similarly, sit in similar positions, and use similar gestures, it can help.

Much of this will have to be done in the interview itself. You can also prepare a bit by looking online for photos that illustrate the company dress code and for videos that show your interviewers in action. While there is no guarantee that you'll be able to get good data, you can check out a company's Facebook page and blog and photos of internal events to get a feel for dress code. You can search on YouTube and Vimeo for your interviewers' names and watch their body language. You can also use tools like PushPin (bitbucket.org/LaNMaSteR53/push-pin), by Tim Tomes, to enter a longitude and latitude (www.findlatitu-deandlongitude.com) and get a listing of photos taken in that area. To run the tool, make sure you have Python loaded, then enter the coordinates and a range. It will open up browser windows with images, videos, and Twitter tweets that are geotagged for that area.

This approach will typically fail for small organizations and will have a high rate of false positives, since even modern smartphones do not always get the geotagging right. However, in larger organizations with campuses, this is a reasonably reliable technique.

Once you know how people in the organization dress, try to dress one level up from the job you wish to have. The meaning of "dress one level up" can be tricky, and this is not a book on fashion. If you, like many, are unclear as to what this means, download the photos into a gallery on a laptop or tablet and take them to a business attire store. Explain what you want to do and ask them to help you. They'll want you to buy a new outfit, of course, and you may want to do so, but either way, it is a very reliable way to find out. Other options include asking people at a fashion program at a nearby college for assistance. Professors may well turn such a question into a topic of discussion for class, though this will depend on your specific school.

It should go without saying that this extends beyond merely clothing. Haircuts, hygiene, and adornments (piercings, tattoos, etc.) should appear in line with the organization's culture.

PLANNING THE CONVERSATIONS

While each interview is theoretically a freeform discussion, you should be guiding it. The interviewers' intention is to decide whether or not to hire you. Your purpose is to decide whether you want them to hire you, and if so, to make it more likely for them to do so. The same boosting technique that was discussed in Chapter 3 applies to discussion as well as the written word.

Interviews are conversations that exist to satisfy curiosity. Your interviewer wants to know about you and has a certain amount of interest in what you have to say. As their curiosity is satisfied, their level of interest in the discussion goes down. To keep the discussion interesting, your job is to add "hooks" to the discussion to re-engage their interest. We do this naturally in interesting conversations with friends, but it's harder to do with strangers.

Fortunately, you've already constructed a metaphor map for these people. This means that you can review your résumé for stories you want to tell and find a way to drop hints in the discussion that tie into your interviewers' metaphors, like baited hooks. If they are picked up on, these hooks can then boost the discussion to a more interesting level. By planting numerous hooks and hoping your interviewer bites on some of them throughout the conversation, you can sustain the level of interest until the interviewer runs out of time. By ending a conversation at a higher level of interest than you started, you increase the likelihood of being invited back or of being offered the job.

For an example on how metaphors are used, reread the previous paragraph with the view of someone who likes to fish. See how the same things are said, but they resonate more strongly to people with a history of fishing. The two figures below illustrate the difference between a conversation with and without hooks.

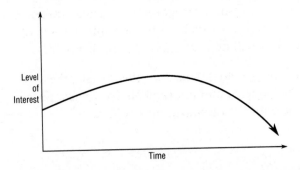

Figure 13.1 Interest Graph—Ordinary Conversations

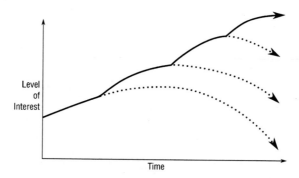

Figure 13.2 Interest Graph—Conversation with Boosting

Suppose you have a story to tell about a time when you were in charge of a system that had performance problems that you solved by sorting through each potential cause until you got to the cause. You have identified that your interviewer is an avid reader of mysteries. By using the phrase "When you have eliminated the impossible, whatever remains, however improbable, must be the truth," you can plant a hook referencing Sherlock Holmes. If the interviewer responds to this, you can use it as a lead-in for your story.

By knowing the metaphors that drive people, you can be prepared with common phrases appropriate to these metaphors. Simply using them will help increase rapport, but by thinking about them ahead of time and linking them to interesting stories, you can go beyond increasing rapport to actively boost the conversation to higher and higher levels. In this model, you are effectively using specific metaphors as springboards. This allows you to logically link the current discussion to something else you wish to discuss, using the metaphorical framework to carry your interviewer along with you as you boost the discussion to more and more interesting topics.

To discover these phrases, search on the subject and "famous quote" or "common phrase," along with variations in conjunction with the metaphor you are exploring. Some examples may help.

Metaphor: *Star Wars*	
Phrase	"I think you overestimate their chances." —Grand Moff Tarkin
Use	Boost to discussing an out-of-touch manager (note, this was used by an evil character, so use carefully)
Phrase	"When 900 years old, you reach. … Look as good, you will not." —Yoda
Use	Boost from discussing migrating from a legacy application to a different, more modern system
Phrase	"You have ____. You have ____. But you don't use them." —Count Dooku
Use	Boost to discussing organization's potential and your role to guide them (note, this was also an evil character)

Metaphor: *Cooking*	
Phrase	"If we're not willing to settle for junk living, we certainly shouldn't settle for junk ____." —Sally Edwards
Use	Boost to discussing core organizational issues and improvement
Phrase	"All happiness depends on a leisurely breakfast." —John Gunther
Use	Boost to discussing the importance of careful planning
Phrase	"A recipe has no soul. You, as the cook, must bring soul to the recipe." —Thomas Keller
Use	Boost to a discussion about programming and style

Metaphor: *Baseball*	
Phrase	"I've tried a lot of things in the off-season, but the only thing I really know is ____." —Hank Aaron
Use	Boost from discussing job changes to discussing the core theme in all the jobs
Phrase	"I wish they'd shut the gates and let us play ball with no press and no fans." —Dick Allen
Use	Boost to discussing the problems with interruptions and the importance of protected time
Phrase	"A wise man once said a baseball takes funny bounces." —Bob Gibson
Use	Boost from discussing job changes to discussing the ultimate goal eventually decided upon

Metaphor: *Military*	
Phrase	"Leadership is the art of getting someone else to do something you want done because he wants to do it." —Dwight Eisenhower
Use	Boost from discussing leadership in general to specific examples
Phrase	"No good decision was ever made in a swivel chair." —George S. Patton
Use	Boost from discussing theory to practice
Phrase	"There are no secrets to success. It is the result of preparation, hard work, learning from failure." —Colin Powell
Use	Boost from an amorphous discussion on career goals to a story about work

Metaphor: *Travel*	
Phrase	"Travel is fatal to prejudice, bigotry, and narrow-mindedness." —Mark Twain
Use	Boost to a discussion of the importance of diversity in a workplace and what you have learned from many projects
Phrase	"There are no foreign lands. It is the traveler only who is foreign." —Robert Louis Stevenson
Use	Boost from a discussion on lack of experience to one of exploration and learning
Phrase	"All journeys have secret destinations of which the traveler is unaware." —Martin Buber
Use	Boost to a discussion about learning

This section makes the concept of boosting sound easier than it often is. This is a very powerful tool but one that is difficult to use successfully. It may be wise to practice with your friends first.

Here is an example conversation that uses two boosting lines, one as a direct quote, the other as reference. In this example, the interviewer (Quinn) has a passing interest in travel but has a military background. The interviewee (Teagan) did research along these lines so the conversation can be controlled.

Quinn: Welcome to Tyrell Corp. Thanks for taking the time to chat with us.

Teagan: It's my pleasure. Thank you for being willing to talk with me.

Quinn: Let's get started. What interests you about this position?

Teagan: Well, I've always been interested in autonomous machinery, and your recent research and development efforts are fascinating.

Quinn: Really? Are you interested in R&D?

Teagan: Well, I view research as a journey, and development as the successful conclusion of that journey. I love the process.

Quinn: Interesting. I'd not heard anyone describe it that way.

Teagan: I like travel. *As Martin Buber said, "All journeys have secret destinations of which the traveler is unaware."* I find that R&D is fun because you get to learn as you go and find ways to help others.

Quinn: You know, that's what got me into this in the first place. I remember when I started and got sent on a trip to Los Angeles ...

... the conversation moves into a rapport-building discussion on work-related travel, having been boosted by the Buber quote ...

Quinn: So, anyway, if we offer you leadership of this team, how would you go about your day? What's your general work style?

Teagan: I think that the important thing is the ultimate goal. Sometimes the goal is best met through a team working together. Sometimes, only one member of the team has the skills to get the work done. I think it's important to delegate the task to them and get the team to pick up their unessential tasks so they can focus. If that person is me, then I'd roll up my sleeves and get to work.

Quinn: So, you'd consider yourself a hands-on manager?

Teagan: Well, as they say, *no good decision was ever made at a desk.* If I put artificial barriers between myself and my team, it's going to get in the way of the goal. That's what matters, after all.

Quinn: That reminds me of my time in the service ...

... the conversation moves into another rapport-building discussion, boosted a second time by a conversational trigger ...

It's important to stress that not everything you plant in a conversation like this will get noticed or picked up on. This example is intentionally blatant to illustrate the point. It's important to realize, though, that even when the conversation is fully directed, the use of familiar language will help your interviewers respond favorably to you. As the conversation moves along, they'll like you more and more, increasing your chances at the job.

Interview: Take Control

It is unusual for a book about job seeking to wait until Chapter 14 to discuss the interview and, once there, to devote such little space to the topic. Fundamentally, by this point, you should be far better prepared than any of your competitors and, in many ways, the interview is less about getting the job than about verifying your assumptions.

THE TRUE PURPOSE OF THE INTERVIEW

The purpose of the interview is for you to learn about the organization and for the organization to learn about you. Your goal is to either get a job directly from the interview or get a second interview with people further up in the hierarchy. That's it. All other things you think an interview is about are distractions. Your thought process should be along these lines:

1. Do I want to do the work?
2. Will I fit into the culture here?
3. Are they willing to pay me enough to compensate for any negatives?
4. Are they willing to pay me enough for me to achieve my financial goals?
5. How can I advance the process?

The reconnaissance process you've gone through to get here should have significantly helped you answer questions 1—4. You should have an idea as to what your expectations are, and you can verify these during the early stages of the interview. You should know what you're willing to accept for compensation and be armed with your total compensation spreadsheet. Once you have validated your assumptions, you're ready to begin advancing the process.

A proper advance will either result in salary negotiation (see Chapter 16) or a plan for the future. Such plans can involve setting up a future interview or receiving a promise to get back to you by a certain date, either with an offer or a future interview. If you cannot get them to commit to a specific date with another step in the process, begin the process with your second choice organization. If the first organization gets its act together, you can always resume the process, but it's imperative not to lose any time while they dither.

SOCIAL NICETIES

Successfully advancing requires using all your tools. The technical tools are easily understood; the softer tools, less so. There are numerous resources online about how to properly shake hands, smile at people, and generally be polite. If you are uncertain how to play these games, educate yourself. In today's world, with all the information available on the Internet, there is no excuse for failing to learn the social languages used by others. You don't have to become an expert, but if you can learn how to manage and manipulate data as the tools listed here allow, you can learn this.

See the Resources section for information on how to read faces and body language.

USING YOUR TOOLS

Throughout this process, you created tools. You have a résumé that lists all the stories you want to tell. You have a portfolio that tells what you've done and what you want to do. Now it's time to use them.

Most interviewers will be ill-prepared for you to effectively take control of their interview and will start as if it's a normal interview. You can save everyone a lot of time if you start the interview by thanking them for the opportunity, telling them that you've prepared some documents for this discussion, and handing out your prepared folders. Alternatively, you can wait until they refer to a copy of your résumé and ask you a question, at which point you can hand them the folder and say, "there's an updated résumé in here, if you wish to use that."

Once the portfolio is out, the game is going to change.

Odds are that they'll still want to ask you some of their prepared questions, but at every opportunity, refer to your additional documents. If they ask you about your past work, show them an example. If they ask you about what you want to do, show them one of the custom documents you created. If they ask you about your hobbies, show them your business card. By tying each verbal question into a visual and verbal response, you make the interaction far more memorable.

If they ask about something for which you've not prepared a document, make one on the fly. The back of your résumé is likely blank, so flip it over and start sketching. If you're in someone's office, ask if you can use his or her whiteboard. Whiteboards are great because they're seldom cleaned until they're needed again. With luck, that person will see their whiteboard and be reminded of your conversation every day until they offer you the job.

Remember that everything in your folders is a tool. It exists for the sole purpose of getting you the job. If that purpose is best filled by you writing on the document, do it. If it requires you to cross things out and adjust the document as you go, so be it. Not only does this further set you apart from everyone else, but it also shows that you understand that ideas must change based on input. A document that you change and then bring back fully updated in a second round of interviews is far more persuasive than a pristine one that just sits on the desk.

Real life is messy; embrace that.

As the interview progresses, you will find things that you'll need to remember, so be sure to bring a notepad. Make notes of anything important that is discussed. This will include things you'll want to use to alter the documents for a second round of interviews, information or links you'll want to send to your interviewers, and anything specific that you'll want to bring up in the thank-you notes.

You should devote one page for each phase of the interview. That is, one page for each person who interviews you or, if you are interviewed by multiple people, for each panel. Each page should have enough information in it that, once you are done with the interview, you can reconstruct the flow of conversation and track any promises and interests. If it has been a while since you've had to take notes, you can practice this skill by taking notes as you watch TV. Once you're at a point where you can understand the important things that were said while jotting down notes, and reconstruct a complete episode from those notes, you'll be in good shape to do it in the actual interview.

MANIPULATING THE CONVERSATION

There has been a lot of focus thus far on pre interview items—tools to use during the interview and how to look and act—but nothing on what to say. That's by design. If you need specific advice on what to say in an interview, get one of those books on how to answer interview questions. By this point, if you've done your research and practiced the common questions, you should be able to have a frank and honest conversation about what the organization needs and how you can help. You don't need any gimmicks or magic answers to inane interview questions. In fact, you should quickly find that you've left all the standard questions behind and are discussing real issues.

That said, there are a few small pointers to the actual discussion.

Setting Schema

First, open with a schema-setting statement. People like to work within structures, and by taking this information- and problem-solving-centered approach, you've blown apart their structure. If you provide them with a new structure, they'll slide into it without stopping to think about what they're doing. One way to do this is with a three-item framing approach.

There are many ways to frame an idea, but in general, people respond well to threes. Think of the three things you want your interviewer to know about you and work those into a sentence or two. Most hiring decisions are made within the first few seconds of meeting someone. The rest of the process is largely about making the decision-makers comfortable with their initial gut-level choice. Framing statements are things like:

- Thanks for meeting with me. I believe that this discussion will help us *both to learn* how I can help you *achieve your goals*. I look forward to discussing your challenges and *collaborating on solutions*.
- I'm glad we were able to connect. I *understand that you have some needs*. I look forward to *learning more* about them and seeing if there's a way we can *work together* in the future.
- I *understand that you're busy*. I've *prepared some documents* to help *speed this process* and make efficient use of both of our time. Shall we get started?

These statements highlight your goals—focus, collaboration, desire to learn and help out, and respect for resources. Once planted, these statements should be revisited at the end of the process to help remind your interviewers about the structure you set up around them so they continue to think in that mode as they work towards their final decision.

Questions and Answers

Questions are asked for two reasons. First, the interviewer genuinely wants to know the answer. Second, the interviewer feels obligated to ask all candidates the same questions out of a sense of fairness or to avoid legal concerns. In general, you'll be able to tell why you're being asked each question by whether the interviewer looks at you or their notes. If they're looking at their notes, you have to find a way to draw them into the conversation. While there are many ways to do this, you can often break the flow by answering the question with a question. Asking for clarification works, but so does trying to work out the meaning behind the question. Be careful how you do this, of course. You don't want to wind up saying things like "It depends on what the meaning of the word 'is' is." However, digging just a little bit deeper is often enough to get people to open up and talk to you.

When answering questions, try to keep answers to definite questions short but phrased in such a way that they lead to more questions. The idea is to slowly work them to one of the stories you have on your résumé. This could take a while, but as you wear them down with short answers and clarifying questions, you can work them off their script.

Once people are off their script, you can begin actually talking. Share your stories and ask for theirs. If they nod at particular parts of your stories, ask if they've been in those situations, too. Ask how they've handled things. Try to understand what their challenges are, and ask what sorts of solutions they've tried. Take notes as you go so you can incorporate this data in future interviews.

If people are talking, they are conveying what matters to them and will necessarily be happier than listening to what matters to you. Sometimes, the best thing you can do in a discussion is leave the other person feeling like they've been heard. Prospective employers want to know that their subordinates will listen to them and take their ideas into consideration when acting. If you are being interviewed by a potential subordinate or coworker, they'll want exactly the same thing. So listen.

Finally, remember that silence is golden. It is fairly common for the quieter person in a discussion to be thought of as the better conversationalist. Don't feel the need to fill the silence with an ill-formed thought. Take the time to think and then answer. During that time, your interviewer may volunteer additional information that will inform your final answer.

Leave Them Wanting More

As discussed in the section on boosting, you'll want to end the interview with your interviewers wanting to know still more about you. If you feel that the interview is getting too complete and you risk satisfying all their curiosity, ask them some questions. Keep the conversation flowing so that their curiosity isn't completely satisfied. Remember, they need a reason to ask you back.

If you feel the conversation is stretching on for too long, feel free to ask your interviewer what his or her schedule looks like. One danger of this approach is that you risk annoying the interviewer by not actually answering his or her questions. You want to keep the conversion moving in a direction, not going around in an indefinite loop.

CHAPTER *15*

Post-Interview: The End of the Interview Is Not the End of the Interview

It is common to believe that the interview ends when you leave the building, but it doesn't. Hopefully, by this point you have had several good conversations, left documents behind, and taken several pages of notes. The rest of the process involves clarifying any misunderstandings, demonstrating adaptability, and following up as needed.

CLARIFICATION EMAILS

If things went well, you were asked things that you didn't know. This is where you do a bit of research and email your interviewers with the answers. If they objected to anything in your documents, this is also where you make corrections, generate PDFs from the updated documents, and attach the files to your emails.

While you should certainly say "thank you" in these emails, these are not thank-you notes. Their purpose is to continue the discussion and make sure that any hanging items that could reflect poorly on you are addressed. This could involve the answer to a technical question that you didn't know, a follow-up to a question of personal interest asked by your interviewer, or a correction to your documentation. These emails should be sent the same day as your interview so your interviewer receives them in the morning when they come into the office. They should also be free of spelling and grammatical errors.

These emails should be simple and to the point, like:

< Name >,

I wanted to thank you for the time you took to visit with me today. You asked a question about Python and I said I'd get back to you. The JSON module was added in Python 2.6. Since Red Hat Enterprise 5.x has Python 2.4 by default, the system will have to have version 2.6 added for native processing of this data type. There are many ways to do this, and the ideal solution will have to be discussed before I can recommend total replacement, side-by-side installation, or a virtual environment.

Additionally, I corrected the typo you found in my "Potential Product Changes" document. Please see the attached PDF for the corrected version.

I look forward to continuing this discussion at our next meeting.

< Your Name >

There's no reason to effuse over their generosity or how much you hope to work with them. That goes in the handwritten thank-you note.

THANK-YOU NOTES

Thank-you notes should be handwritten and personalized. This does not mean that you should start writing them out by hand. Each should be different, not based on a template, but should be short enough to fit in a single thank-you note. You can draft them in a word processor first, to get your spelling and grammar checks in, then transcribe them to the notecard. Your handwriting should be legible and avoid unnecessary flourishes. After all, you're not going after a job writing letters. You need to express your thoughts succinctly so you don't waste your interviewers' time.

Focus the notes on thanking your interviewers, mentioning a specific reference or two to the discussion, and closing with an appropriate ending. Some examples follow:

< Name >
Thank you for taking the time to have an exploratory discussion about your products. I enjoyed it very much and hope that you agree there are interesting things we could do together. The "slope" drawing I made has the official name "cumulative flow diagram" and is part of queuing theory. I have sent you additional information about this via email.
Thanks again,
< Your Name >

< Name >

I wanted to thank you once again for meeting with me and being willing to accelerate the pace of our discussions. It sounds to me as if we are very strongly aligned in our goals and capabilities. The discussion around growing the market was particularly enjoyable. I am greatly looking forward to meeting with you again on < Date > so we can finalize the next phase of working together.

Looking forward to the future,

< Your Name >

< Name >

Thank you, once again, for treating me to lunch. I very much enjoyed our discussion, and as I think about it, I would be interested in exploring opportunities in the education market. As there is a long sales cycle and we have discussed focusing on other verticals first, I would like to begin laying the groundwork there and possibly make it an area of focus at some point in the future.

Respectfully,

< Your Name >

Each example is of similar size and can be written out fairly easily. Once done, address each note, add a stamp, and drop them in the mail the following day. The idea is for them to arrive within a few days of the interview to remind people that you were there and that you had some good discussions.

CHECKING IN

If you were told that you'd hear back by a specific date, wait one day past that date, then send a polite email to your contact asking for a status update. Then wait two more days; if you still haven't heard from them, send an email to the person with whom you most connected during the interview. If you still haven't heard after a couple more days, telephone your contact. If you can't reach them, call the person with whom you best connected. If you still can't get any answers, it's time to move to the next organization on your list.

If you do get an answer, adjust your time frame accordingly and basically reset the clock. Just remember to be polite and understand that their mental clock will almost always run slower than yours. After all, you want to start something new or have an existing opening adjusted to better meet your needs. However, in order for you to do so, the organization has to prepare a space for you, find budget, allocate training time, and determine whether the cash flow will support your hiring. That's almost always going to take longer than expected, especially if you demonstrate that you're better than they were expecting.

Remember, this process is designed to shake things up. It's going to take a bit of time for things to fall back into place before things can move forward.

REVISING YOUR PORTFOLIO

If it looks as if there will be follow-up interviews, update your documents from the notes you took in your discussions. You should have already fixed the deliberate errors that you added to the documents, so you could send the updated versions out via email. This is the point in the process where you review them for missing structure. Perhaps you made a guess as to how the organization functions and missed an entire use case. Perhaps you believed the organization did something it no longer does and need to remove aspects of your documents.

Hopefully, you got brand-new ideas and want to make new documents detailing your ideas. While you wait for your next interview or to hear whether you're getting a next interview, spend some time being creative. That way, when you go in again, you can do the portfolio trick again with both updated and new documents in it. This will demonstrate that you are learning and moving forward.

If, at the end of your waiting period, it turns out that you will not be moving forward, you can use your learning to help bootstrap your process with another organization.

SUBSEQUENT INTERVIEWS

If you succeed in getting a follow-up interview, preparation will go just as before. Quickly run through the process again, using the information you got from the interview to make additional searches and preparation. Update the personal cheat sheets so you can remember more about your interviewers. Create data sheets for any new people you may need to interview with.

Then, when it comes time for the interview, you should be able to do even better. Remember, the point of subsequent interviews is usually to get other people in the organization to buy in to their creating a new position for you. If you come in for a second round, at least one person in the organization wants to hire you, and you just have to win over a few others. Keep at it, and so long as each interview is with another set of people and advances the process, it's worth doing.

CHAPTER 16

Salary Negotiation: Everything Can Be Flexible

This chapter addresses the point in the process where your target has offered you a job and you are evaluating the offer. In general, the question you should be asking yourself is how flexible they are. If they are willing to be flexible, it's worth negotiating. If they're more of a "take it or leave it" organization, your decision is simple. If you think the job is worth what they'll be paying you to do, take it. If not, tell them that you can't change jobs without a better offer and thank them for their time. It's possible they'll change their offer, but that's up to them. You're not playing a game here. If you turn them down, you have to be serious about it and ready to move on to the next target organization on your list.

This is not intended to be a complete guide to salary negotiation. There are other works devoted to that topic. Instead, you should read this section to get ideas, then use other sources to delve deeper into them.

WORKING WITH TOTAL COMPENSATION

The key idea behind the total compensation calculation you ran earlier is that what you take home in terms of money is only part of what an organization gives you in exchange for your work. The total compensation approach captures less-tangible items like ongoing education and health care benefits. In many organizations, the budget these things come out of is different from the one that pays salary, so if they can't boost your actual salary, they may be able to do other things for you. These things generally fall into "financial" and "nonfinancial" benefits.

Financial Benefits

A financial benefit is one that involves money. There are more ways to get money than just your paycheck. Different industries vary in how much they employ such methods; but in general, the higher you rise within an organization's hierarchy, the less your compensation plan looks like a simple hourly or salaried rate, and the more confusing it gets.

Hiring Bonus

The simplest form of financial benefit is the hiring bonus. These come in different forms, from a lump-sum payment to lure you away from your current employer to ways to defray your costs in taking the new job. This can show up as a traditional bonus like relocation assistance. However, it can also take alternative forms such as training for a technology you need to do the job or reimbursement for a certification you paid for yourself in order to land the job. Not all organizations will do this, but for those that do, it can be very helpful to have receipts that demonstrate that the costs you claim are legitimate.

Stock

In general, stock is a share in the company that you can cash in at some future time. An alternate form of this approach is a stock option, which gives you the ability to purchase stock at a set price at some point in the future.

Stock and stock options are usually given on a vesting schedule, so the value doesn't truly materialize until you've been employed for a given period of time. When negotiating based on total compensation, remember that stock values fluctuate, so look at a five-year average to pick a reasonable estimate on value. Then, if the stock vests, spread the value out over the vesting period. For example, a stock offer worth $10,000 that vests in five years is actually worth $2,000 per year. If it vested in two years, it would be worth $5,000 per year.

Performance Pay

Performance pay is another form of bonus, but it is paid after a period of time, not at hiring, and it tends to come in three flavors. Individualized performance pay is based directly on how well you do your job. This is typically for people who are considered "billable resources," where you get to keep a fraction of the amount of money you bill out. This can be done as a fraction of the total amount billed or a fraction of the margin made on your billing rate. Either is reasonable, but be sure to run some calculations to verify that whatever option is presented will be acceptable. Salespeople tend to live largely on their commissions, with a very low base salary. This is typically reversed for technical people. If a large percentage of your salary is expected to be based on a commission, it may be wise to consider aspects outside of your control, such as how much interest salespeople have in selling your services, support from marketing people, the maximum amount of work you can sustain over time, and how much time you spend working "after hours." If you find that the estimates do not match what is being discussed, it's worth running through the calculations with the organization and seeing if they can raise the fraction that goes to you to make up for overly optimistic calculations.

Group performance pay is much like individual performance pay, but it is focused on rewarding the team. In these models, the team is often given group goals that, if met, result in a lump-sum payment to be divided among the team. Sometimes this is divided relatively fairly (equal or apportioned according to effort or seniority), and sometimes it's up to the manager to adjust it. The group approach to performance pay should work well in theory, but in practice it can fail due (among other reasons) to small teams simply not being given the resources to succeed. As with any performance-based structure, be sure that you are provided with what you need to reach your goals.

Organizational performance pay is more common in large organizations and is referred to as profit sharing. If the organization makes a profit, the money is shared among the staff, often as a flat percentage of salary. This results in managers receiving the largest amount of the organization's profit, then salaried employees, and finally hourly workers. It's worth noting that some organizations receive significant tax benefits by failing to make a profit in some years. In such years, no organizational bonuses would be available, though individual and group performance pay might still be an option.

While there are many ways to make performance pay work well in theory, it does not always do so in practice, so be careful to research ways in which the model might fail before you agree to such a plan.

Nonfinancial Benefits

Nonfinancial benefits include less-tangible things. Educational options, such as a certain amount of money made available for college classes, conferences, or training, can be extremely beneficial, but only if you qualify for and use them. This money can be used to gain degrees or certifications and, ideally, to sustain them. When working this into your total compensation calculation, consider how much you would actually use on a yearly basis. After all, not everyone has the time in their personal lives to take full advantage of courses. If you want to negotiate for more, do so by all means, but only if truly you plan to take advantage of it.

Time off is another benefit to consider. Many different models exist, from a simple paid time off (PTO) model in which an employee accumulates days off at a certain rate, to highly complex systems that combine personal days, vacation days, and sick days. In general, calculate your days off at your daily rate and add them to your base salary. For example, if you are going for a $50,000/year job with two weeks of vacation, that indicates that each day is worth $192.31 ($50,000 divided by 52 weeks, divided by five work days in each week). Thus, your two weeks of paid vacation is worth $1,923.10 ($192.31 times two weeks times five days per week). This sets your base salary at $51,923.10, at least for comparison purposes. This way, the complexities involved in time rollover and converting between sick and personal time all go away, as all time is represented as dollars.

When it comes time to negotiate, you can find a lot of flexibility in terms of days off. Using days off as a negotiation point can allow you to devote entire weeks to advancing your work life (after all, you did just make them create a job for you, so you'd better deliver) with the certainty that you'll be able to take time for yourself at some point in the future.

One other common benefit, at least in the US, is that of health benefits. Different organizations have different plans that vary by employee share, employer share, co-pay, dental, eye, etc. It's easy to compare plans based on total features, but it's much harder to evaluate them based on which features you are likely to use. Since insurance is a hedge against future losses, and you don't know the future, some guesswork is required. Also, health benefits are often nonnegotiable, as they are a group purchase. Just factor them into your total compensation plan and decide if you can live under such a health plan.

NEGOTIATING BASICS

If you believe the deal you are looking at is unfair but worth the attempt to make it more fair, it's time to negotiate. While there are all sorts of tricks to use in a one-time negotiation to get your way, it may be best to not use any of them here. Unlike the other tips contained herein, compensation negotiation has effects that last for the length of your entire employment. If you push too hard, you risk souring the relationship before it even starts. Instead, consider three simple rules:

1. Be fair
2. Know when to stop
3. Keep the organization's needs in mind

Be Fair

The goal is not to hold your negotiating partner over a barrel, unless you plan to leave and find a new job in a year or two. Frame all your discussions in terms of what is fair and what you need, not what you want. Some people want more money just to have more money. A fair negotiation would focus on what money is needed. For example, if you have to have more money to pay for a health care assistant for an ailing parent, you can frame it as "It is what it is, and nothing you or I do can change it. I either need enough extra salary to pay for an assistant, or I need more time off so I can pay the assistant less and do more of the work myself. I don't want to be greedy, but my parent's well-being means more to me than this job; so if I can't take care of them, I'll have to pass on the offer."

That is a straightforward presentation of facts that is difficult to argue with. When framed in this way, your negotiating partner can either help you out or not. If they can't, you can part as friends; and if they can, you can get the compensation you need, either as salary or time off.

Know When to Stop

The classic work on negotiation *Getting to YES* introduces the concept of the best alternative to a negotiated agreement (BATNA). The core idea here is to identify, before you enter negotiation, what your exit option is. Perhaps it's continuing to work where you currently are. Perhaps it is getting a less interesting job at a better rate of pay. Perhaps it's going freelance for a period of time. Whatever you're going to do if this negotiation falls through, figure out what its worth is, and if the negotiation falls below this BATNA, be prepared to stop negotiations and move on to other options.

Keep the Organization's Needs in Mind

Your future organization is talking to you for one simple reason: They think they'll be more successful with you than without you. Keep this in mind at all times. If the negotiation starts to lean too far in your direction, it will eventually cross an invisible line, and the organization will be better off without you. The goal is to grow with your organization, not start off with an adversarial relationship. By focusing on this facet of the negotiation, you can work together to find a solution that works for both of you.

ACCEPTING OR REJECTING THE OFFER

Once you and the organization have both settled on an agreement, you must formally accept the offer. This will protect you once you give notice at your current firm, if applicable. You may initially accept it verbally, but you must accept it in writing in order to get the protection you need. Make certain, before you sign it, that the offer letter you receive includes each point you negotiated. Some organizations may try a bait and switch on you. Others manage to screw up the terms because different departments work on different parts of the letter. It's rare, but it does happen.

You should also send a quick thank-you note to each person who helped you along the way. This keeps your network alive should you need to use it in the future.

If you decide to reject the offer, do so carefully and in such a way as to keep your options open. If you don't think you'd be a good fit, mention that, but do so without bad-mouthing the organization. Try to have a reason that isn't something they can or were willing to negotiate. Perhaps you like large companies and want to focus on a narrower range of tasks than a small business can afford and the offered salary doesn't compensate for that change. Perhaps you need more time with your family than the culture allows and while the salary is fine, they can't be flexible with respect to time. That's why total compensation should be considered; it allows you to press for advantage during negotiation but also to bow out without burning bridges in a way that both parties understand. It's reasonable to want something different than what they offer. That is, after all, why different organizations exist.

CHAPTER 17

Giving Notice: Parting Is Such Sweet Sorrow

The final piece of your job search, unless you are unemployed, is giving notice to your current company. While you likely do not need to dig deep into indicators as to how your organization functions, it can be useful to know how they are likely to respond. Some will be very understanding and help you in many ways, from adjusting your departure date to maximizing your insurance coverage to requesting that you remain available should they need you in an emergency. Others will consider the risk too great and walk you out the door immediately. You will probably already have a feel for which of these is most likely to happen, based on how your organization has treated others in your situation. It is also likely to vary according to how reliant they are on you.

If you know all of the passwords and are deeply involved in the organization's infrastructure, you may be walked out the door immediately—but only if there is another person in the organization who also knows these things. If there is not, you will probably be treated with kid gloves while the organization makes sure that it can function without you. The same goes for people with deep product or operations knowledge. You can make your best guess as to which scenario you face, but your employer will decide what to do. To best protect yourself, you should prepare for the worst.

PREPARING FOR THE WORST

Barring situations in which you've been caught engaging in illegal or unethical activities, the worst that will happen when you give notice is that you'll be escorted off the property and HR will send you your belongings at a later date. This is easily handled. After all, you've known for a while that you were planning to leave, so you should have been gradually removing your belongings from your work area. If you have sufficient time, make it look like you're just cleaning up so you don't inadvertently cause other people to guess what you're planning. Then, the day before you plan to give notice, take the last of your personal stuff home so you are ready to go the next morning if you have to.

Though it is certainly possible to take digital copies of files, source code, and other items that may technically belong to the organization, doing so is generally frowned upon and may result in negative consequences. Think about this carefully and consider purging any "backups" that may exist on your personal media. Be careful, though, not to destroy your public work. Anything you did to create your portfolio should be fair game and able to be kept in perpetuity.

BENEFITS

Insurance issues will vary depending on where you live, where you work, and where you're going. In the United States, where it is common to have health insurance tied to employment, it is often wise to make sure that your last official day at your current organization is the first of the month. This extends your benefits for a month while the waiting period at your new organization is in effect. In some cases, it might be feasible for you to take some personal time to extend your stay at your old organization while you start at your new one near the end of the last month. This minimizes your wait time while extending your old company's benefits. If you can't work the timing perfectly, you may wish to consider getting private health insurance to cover your gap in coverage. Your local insurance agent can assist you with this. If you're in the US, you can also play the retroactive COBRA insurance game. The HR department of your new organization should be able to explain how this works.

Another benefit to consider is that of retirement savings. Retirement vehicles like 401(k) plans and pension plans have specific rules as to what happens to the money after you are no longer associated with the organization. Usually, the money you put in is yours, and that of your employer is vested according to a specific schedule. There are ways in which you can convert your funds to similar retirement accounts at little or no loss to you. However, these methods change from year to year as tax and related laws change. See a financial adviser for specific suggestions around this issue.

GOTCHAS

There are some areas in which leaving your current organization can create problems for you. Ideally, you should have considered these issues before starting this book, but it's a good idea to think about such things again before you enter the formal exit negotiation process.

Noncompete Agreements

The biggest thing that affects most people in this situation is a non-compete agreement. There is a general belief in the information technology community that noncompete agreements are non-enforceable and that there is no reason to worry about them. However, even though an agreement is going to be struck down by a court, the mere fact that it gets to court could cost you significant money and possibly cause your new organization to withdraw its offer. The rules as to what a noncompete can and cannot require, and what a hiring organization can and cannot do to withdraw an offer of employment, vary from state to state and country to country. If you have a noncompete agreement with your current organization, it is best to consult with a lawyer specializing in employment law.

Often, though, such noncompetes may be negotiated as part of your exit strategy. As you review your agreement, look at how it defines your work, your industry, the geographical region and time frame in which you are banned from working, and any customer and employee relationships. For example, suppose an agreement reads as follows:

"Upon leaving employment, employee is prohibited from providing information technology services to any company, for profit or nonprofit, within the United States for the period of three years. Additionally, the employee is prohibited from soliciting any customers, employees, former customers, or former employees for a period of five years."

This is the sort of language that is overly broad and considered non-enforceable. However, such non-enforceability is often dependent on a good-faith effort to change the agreement. You can suggest an alteration of the language to do any of the following:

- Reduce the definition of "information technology" to something more specific, such as "database management" or "VB.NET development."
- Reduce the geographical scope from "United States" to a state or city.
- Reduce the time frame from three years to one.
- Reduce the "any customers" scope to "any customers the employee has contacted in the last year."

If these restrictions are offered and accepted, there is nothing to worry about. If they are rejected, you have prepared your case for a legal battle, if needed.

Intellectual Property

Intellectual property restrictions are often intended to prevent you from taking source code, client data, or process documents to a competitor. However, they are often written to also claim any work you do at any time. Such agreements can attempt to claim ownership of personal projects, open source projects, or any books, articles, or blog posts you may create. Since part of this process involves doing more public work, it is hoped that you have considered these issues ahead of time. If you did not, and you believe that such restrictions are likely to cause you problems, you can renegotiate such agreements as you exit your current employment. Following a similar process as with non-competes, consult with an intellectual property lawyer first. Then, with his or her help, begin to reduce the scope of what is claimed where you can, specifically calling out rights and ownership of specific works you wish to retain. It may help to conduct a reconnaissance process against yourself to uncover any works you may have forgotten about.

FORMAL PROCESS

You should give notice in person if you can, but always give your notice in writing. If you are leaving because you are upset or angry, using a letter helps to keep emotion out of it. If you really like the people you have worked with, even though it's appropriate for you to leave, this can also help to keep you from losing control over more positive emotions. The letter should be short and simple. It should simply explain that you are leaving and give the effective date. If you wish to negotiate at all, you should mention that your notice period is negotiable, as is your postemployment availability. Keep it short and sweet.

NEGOTIATING NOTICE

If you intend to ask for additional consideration from your soon-to-be-former organization, first determine what you want, such as being let out of a contractual obligation or an extension of benefits. From this, consider the minimum and maximum amount of time you are willing to stay and whether you are willing to work evenings and weekends to facilitate the transition. If it's worth it to you and practical with regard to your new employer, consider extending the standard two-week notice period to three or four weeks. This will, in theory, give your current organization a chance to hire someone to replace you and give you time to train them. Though this offer is frequently made and accepted, organizations seldom take advantage of it.

Another point of consideration is what rate you plan to charge your soon-to-be-former organization for assistance on a freelance basis and whether your future organization will let you bill them yourself or if it would have to go through them. If the future organization will effectively be contracting you back to your former organization, you need to get them to let you know what this rate will be. This hourly rate should cover your cost to your future company plus a slight profit on your time. The rate should be sufficiently low as to appear a good deal to them so you can use it for negotiation. Such rates, if offered, should be limited from a time perspective, lest you risk continuing to work for your former employer. Typically, this is phrased as: "In exchange for reducing the noncompete term from three years to one year, employee agrees to work upon request for the company at $80/hr. This will be billed by New Company, and the rate will remain in force for a period of one year."

If freelancing is an option that was agreed to by your future employer, consider what rate is worth your time to do work for them. If you haven't done freelance work before, double your original estimate and use that as a negotiation item. A good rule of thumb is to start with the highest number you can say out loud with a straight face.

COUNTEROFFERS

It may be that your current employer offers you more money or benefits to stay. While the ultimate decision is up to you, in almost all cases the correct decision is to decline such an offer. Accepting the counteroffer would sour the relationship with the new organization that you have just spent a significant amount of time developing; and the fact that you gave notice will have soured your relationship with your current employer. Additional money can be good, but accepting a counteroffer is a trick you can usually play only once. And once it has been played, your employment situation will grow far more uncomfortable and will be unlikely to improve.

EXIT INTERVIEW

Everything mentioned here should be settled well in advance of the obligatory exit interview with your current employer. It's always tempting to use these interviews as your chance to "set the record straight" and tell everyone what you really think of them. However, all this approach does is harm you. If you could have changed the organization, you would have done so while working there. In this interview, be polite and relatively noncommittal. Make sure they know that you enjoyed working there but that it's time to move on. Then, move on.

CHAPTER 18

Conclusion

In the end, information only takes you so far. You will not get a job simply by knowing things or making good guesses about people's personal proclivities. Information is only useful if it is actually used.

It is common for people to be nervous when job hunting. Increased familiarity—with the interviewers, with the organization's needs, and with the process as a whole—helps calm the nerves and allows you to shine in interviews. The world is full of people who interview well but can't do the work. By going through this process, you can demonstrate the most important criterion—that you can do the work. It takes a truly stupendous effort of will to examine your ethics, exhaustively research people and organizations, discover their metaphors, and adjust your résumé, cover letter, and additional documents to meet their needs. Once this is done, you have to communicate your work to others, which involves social understanding, discussion, and visualization skills. Then, you must negotiate the legal morasses of contract law. And if you currently have a job, you have to do all of this in your off-hours. It's a lot of work, but when it all comes together, the result can be almost magical.

As with all work, there will be hurdles. Not every company you target will give you an interview. Not every interview will land you a job. However, each time you go through the process, you will learn more and the overall process will get easier. As time goes by, you will be able to learn more quickly and improve your skills. As your preparation, writing, presentation, and interview skills develop, you will rise in corporate hierarchies, negotiate salary and benefits more effectively, and—most importantly—have more interesting work to do.

Really, that's what important. Work is about helping others. Economies are (for the most part) founded on this concept. If you're not providing value to someone, there's no reason to pay you. The information you uncover can allow you to work the process to your advantage, but it can also allow you to shortcut areas of miscommunication, identify what is truly needed, and focus on helping you and your organization grow together. When you succeed in these, your life can become amazingly wonderful. You have no idea what is in store for you, but it's going to be an adventure.

Best of luck to you.

Resources

This book discussed a great many resources. Additionally, there were many that could simply not be covered. This appendix contains all resources listed within the book as well as others that you may wish to review yourself.

SEARCH RESOURCES

There are many types of search resources. It is likely that you are familiar with the basic ones listed here, but for deep and niche searches, additional tools will be needed. Also listed are tools that allow for automated searching, searching the future and past, and tools to find additional keywords to broaden your searching.

Basic Searching
- Ask—ask.com
- Bing—bing.com
- Blekko—www.blekko.com
- Duck Duck Go—duckduckgo.com
- Google—google.com
- Ixquick—ixquick.com
- Yacy—yacy.net
- Yahoo—yahoo.com
- Yandex—yandex.com
- Yippy—search.yippy.com

Search Filters and Manipulations
- Bing Operators—msdn.microsoft.com/en-us/library/ff795620.aspx
- *Google Hacking Volumes 1 and 2* by Long and others—1931836361 and 978597491761
- *Google Hacks: Tips & Tools for Finding and Using the World's Information* by Dornfest, Bausch, and Calishain—0596527063
- Google Operators—googleguide.com/advanced_operators_reference .html

- Yahoo Operators—www.creativeconfusion.net/search_engines/yahoo-commands.html

Deep Searching
- Ark—ark.com
- Clusty—clusty.com
- Complete Planet—aip.completeplanet.com
- Contracting & Organizations Research Institute—cori.missouri.edu
- Deep Web Listing—deep-web.org/how-to-research/deep-web-search-engines
- Entity Cube—entitycube.research.microsoft.com
- Market Visual—www.marketvisual.com
- NNDB—nndb.com
- NNDB Mapper—mapper.nndb.com
- PeopleFinders—www.peoplefinders.com
- Scirus—scirus.com
- Search Engine Guide—www.searchengineguide.com/searchengines.html
- Social—so.cl
- Social Mention—socialmention.com
- Spokeo—www.spokeo.com
- Wolfram Alpha—www.wolframalpha.com

Niche Searches
- Bing Events Search—www.bing.com/events/search
- FollowTheMoney—www.followthemoney.org
- Glassdoor—www.glassdoor.com
- Google Blog Search—www.google.com/blogsearch
- Google Code—code.google.com
- Google Groups—groups.google.com
- Google Maps—maps.google.com
- Google News search—news.google.com
- Google Patent Search—www.google.com/?tbm = pts
- LittleSis—littlesis.org
- Open Secrets—OpenSecrets.org
- PushPin—bitbucket.org/LaNMaSteR53/pushpin

Automated Searching
- eSearchy—github.com/FreedomCoder/esearchy
- eSearchy-ng—github.com/FreedomCoder/ESearchy-ng
- eSearchy-mirai—github.com/FreedomCoder/esearchy_mirai

- Fierce—ha.ckers.org/fierce
- Fierce2—trac.assembla.com/fierce
- FOCA—www.informatica64.com/foca.aspx
- Maltego by Paterva—www.paterva.com/web6/products/maltego.php
- NameChk—namechk.com
- Recon-ng—bitbucket.org/LaNMaSteR53/recon-ng/wiki/Home
- Scythe—github.com/ChrisJohnRiley/Scythe
- The Harvester—code.google.com/p/theharvester
- Threat Agent—www.threatagent.com

Searching the Future
- Google Trends—www.google.com/trends
- Recorded Future—www.recordedfuture.com
- Silobreaker—www.silobreaker.com
- Trends Map—trendsmap.com
- What the Trend—whatthetrend.com
- Yahoo Trending Now—news.yahoo.com/blogs/trending-now

Searching the Past
- Google Cache—google.com (click "cached button")
- Internet Archive's Wayback Machine—archive.org/web/web.php
- NeoDiggler—addons.mozilla.org/en-us/firefox/addon/neo-diggler

Search Suggesters
- Google Keywords—adwords.google.com/o/KeywordTool
- MW Thesaurus—www.merriam-webster.com/dictionary/thesaurus
- SEO Book—tools.seobook.com/keyword-tools/seobook
- SEO Central—www.seocentro.com
- Thesaurus.com—thesaurus.com
- Uber Suggest—ubersuggest.org
- Visual Thesaurus—www.visualthesaurus.com
- WordTracker—freekeywords.wordtracker.com

Business-specific Search
- Book of Lists—www.bookoflistsonline.com
- Google Finance—www.google.com/finance
- Hoover's—hoovers.com
- Jigsaw—jigsaw.com
- RapLeaf—rapleaf.com
- SEC filings site—www.secinfo.com
- Yahoo Finance—finance.yahoo.com

HIDING YOUR IDENTITY

- Golden Frog's VyperVPN—www.goldenfrog.com/vyprvpn
- HideMyAss!—hidemyass.com
- IPVanish—www.ipvanish.com
- Rise Up—riseup.net/en
- Tor—www.torproject.org

MANAGING THE PROCESS

Any book of this nature must be misleading. In order for the process to make sense to the reader, it must flow logically. In real life, however, things don't quite move so smoothly. Your time can be consumed by all sorts of things, from your current job to family crises to writer's block or just plain distraction. To succeed, you must be able to manage your time, manage your tasks, and create the documents that you'll need for the actual interview.

Time Management
- Focus Booster—www.focusboosterapp.com/live
- *Getting Things Done: The Art of Stress-Free Productivity* by Allen—0142000280
- Kimai—www.kimai.org/en
- *Personal Kanban: Mapping Work | Navigating Life* by Benson and Barry—1453802266
- Project Hamster—projecthamster.wordpress.com/about
- Rescue Time—www.rescuetime.com
- *The 7 Habits of Highly Effective People* by Covey—0743269519
- *The Dip* by Godin—9781591841661
- *The Now Habit* by Fiore—1585425524
- Tomato—http://tomato.es

Task Management
- Google Tasks—mail.google.com/mail/help/tasks
- Outlook Tasks
- Remember the Milk—www.rememberthemilk.com
- Tasque—wiki.gnome.org/Tasque
- Trello—trello.com
- Wunderlist—www.6wunderkinder.com/wunderlist

Data Management
- Bookmark Trackers
  - Delicious—delicious.com
  - Diigo—diigo.com
  - Pinboard—pinboard.in
- Mind Mappers
  - Bubbl.us—bubbl.us
  - Coggle—coggle.it
  - FreeMind—freemind.sourceforge.net/wiki/index.php/Main_Page
  - Mind 42—mind42.com
  - Mind Meister—www.mindmeister.com
  - XMind—www.xmind.net
- Note Takers
  - EverNote—evernote.com
  - Google Keep—drive.google.com/keep
  - OneNote—office.microsoft.com/en-us/onenote
  - Soho Notes—www.chronosnet.com/Products/sohonotes.html
  - Spring Pad—springpad.com
  - Zotero—www.zotero.org
- RSS Readers
  - Bloglines—www.bloglines.com
  - Digg Reader—digg.com/reader
  - Feedly—cloud.feedly.com
  - The Old Reader—theoldreader.com

Graphic Design
- Colors
  - Colllor—colllor.com
  - Color Combos Color Grabber—www.colorcombos.com/grab colors.html
  - Color Palette Generator—www.degraeve.com/color-palette
  - Color Scheme Designer—colorschemedesigner.com
- Fonts
  - Font Picker—www.fontpicker.net
  - Julian Hansen's Font Choice—julianhansen.com/files/infographi-clarge_v2.png
  - Klixo Font Chooser—klixo.com/tools/font_chooser.html
  - Wordmark—wordmark.it

- Layout Tools
  - Gimp—www.gimp.org
  - Inkscape—Inkscape.org
  - LibreOffice—www.libreoffice.org
  - Scribus—www.scribus.net/canvas/Scribus
- Reference Sources
  - Bing Images—www.bing.com/images
  - Creative Commons—search.creativecommons.org
  - Exalead—www.exalead.com/search/image
  - Flickr Search—www.flickr.com/search
  - Google Image Search—www.google.com/imghp
  - Pinterest Visual Résumés—pinterest.com/rtkrum/infographic-visual-resumes
  - TinEye Reverse Image Search—www.tineye.com
  - Visualize Me—vizualize.me
  - Yahoo Images—images.search.yahoo.com

MANAGING MONEY

There are many ways to manage your money, and this is not a book on personal finance. However, it may be useful to look up more information on negotiation, cost of living, and places to go for help for the things you can't do yourself.

Negotiation
- *Getting to YES: Negotiating Agreement without Giving In* by Fisher, Ury, and Patton—0143118757
- *How to Read a Person Like a Book* by Nierenberg, Calero, and Grayson—9780757003141
- *The Art of Negotiating* by Nierenberg—156619816X

Cost of Living Calculators
- CNN—money.cnn.com/calculator/pf/cost-of-living
- Best Places—www.bestplaces.net/cost-of-living/
- BankRate—bankrate.com/calculators/savings/moving-cost-of-living-calculator.aspx
- Payscale—www.payscale.com/cost-of-living-calculator
- Salary.com—swz.salary.com/costoflivingwizard/layoutscripts/coll_start.aspx

Getting Help
- CE-L freelancers list—www.copyediting-l.info
- FedEx Office—www.fedex.com/us/office
- OfficeDepot Copy and Print—www.officedepot.com/a/design-print-and-ship
- OfficeMax Print Center—www.officemax.com/home/custom.jsp?id=m9540558

SOCIAL SKILLS

You are not going to develop/improve your social skills overnight. However, unless you begin the process of improvement, nothing will change. Start developing your social skills, not for the job you bought this book to get, but for the job after that.

Networking Keywords
- "BNI"
- "Chamber of Commerce Events"
- "Jaycees"
- "Networking"
- "Rotary"
- "Toastmasters"
- "User Group <subject of interest>"

Communication and General Improvement
- *Definitive Book of Body Language* by Pease and Pease—0553804723
- *Emotions Revealed: Recognizing Faces and Feelings to Improve Communication and Emotional Life* by Ekman—0805083391
- *How to Win Friends and Influence People* by Carnegie—1439167346
- *On Writing Well: The Classic Guide to Writing Nonfiction* by Zinsser—0060006641
- *Orbiting the Giant Hairball: A Corporate Fool's Guide to Surviving with Grace* by MacKenzie—0670879835
- *Presentation Zen: Simple Ideas on Presentation Design and Delivery* by Reynolds—0321811984
- *slide:ology: The Art and Science of Creating Great Presentations* by Duarte—0596522347
- *Social Engineering: The Art of Human Hacking* by Hadnagy—0470639539

- *What Every BODY Is Saying: An Ex-FBI Agent's Guide to Speed-Reading People* by Navarro and Karlins—0061438294
- *Writing as Thinking* by Jacobus—0023601604

Interviewing and Job Hunting Techniques
- *201 Best Questions to Ask on Your Interview* by Kador—0071387730
- *60 Seconds and You're Hired!* by Ryan—0143112902
- *Brag!: The Art of Tooting Your Own Horn without Blowing It* by Klaus—0446692786
- *Cracking the Coding Interview: 150 Programming Questions and Solutions* by McDowell—098478280X
- *Don't Send a Resume: And Other Contrarian Rules to Help Land a Great Job* by Fox—0786865962
- *How to Land Your Dream Job: No Resume! and Other Secrets to Get You in the Door* by Fox—1401303048
- *How Would You Move Mount Fuji?: Microsoft's Cult of the Puzzle – How the World's Smartest Companies Select the Most Creative Thinkers* by Poundstone—0316778494
- *Nail the Job Interview!: 101 Dynamite Answers to Interview Questions* by Krannich and Krannich—1593160232

Storytelling and Metaphor
- *I Is an Other: The Secret Life of Metaphor and How It Shapes the Way We See the World* by Geary—9780061710292
- *Images of Organization* by Morgan—1412939798
- *Made to Stick: Why Some Ideas Survive and Others Die* by Heath and Heath—1400064287
- *Master Metaphor List v2*–Lakoff, Espenson, Goldberg, and Schwartz—araw.mede.uic.edu/~alansz/metaphor/METAPHORLIST.pdf
- *Metaphors We Live By* by Lakoff and Johnson—0226468011
- *Pixar Story Rules* by Coats—filmmakeriq.com/2012/08/the-pixar-story-rules
- *Story: Substance, Structure, Style, and the Principles of Screenwriting* by McKee—9780060391683
- *The Golden Theme: How to Make Your Writing Appeal to the Highest Common Denominator* by McDonald—0984178678
- *The Seven Basic Plots: Why We Tell Stories* by Booker—0826480373

- *The Stuff of Thought: Language as a Window into Human Nature* by Pinker—0143114247
- *The War of Art: Break Through the Blocks and Win Your Inner Creative Battles* by Pressfield—1936891026
- *Visual Explanations: Images and Quantities, Evidence and Narrative* by Tufte—0961392126
- *Visual Story Lab's 2013 Report*—www.resource-media.org/visual-story-lab/report
- *Whoever Tells the Best Story Wins: How to Use Your Own Stories to Communicate with Power and Impact* by Simmons—0814409148
- *Wired for Story: The Writer's Guide to Using Brain Science to Hook Readers from the Very First Sentence* by Cron—1607742454

Privacy Lockdown
- Facebook—www.facebook.com/settings/?tab = privacy&privacy_source = settings_menu
- Google—www.google.com/goodtoknow/online-safety/security-tools/
- LinkedIn—www.linkedin.com/settings/
- LiveJournal—www.livejournal.com/manage/settings/?cat = privacy
- Microsoft—www.microsoft.com/security/online-privacy/overview.aspx
- MySpace—www.myspace.com/my/settings/account/privacy
- SimpleWash—simplewa.sh
- Twitter—twitter.com/settings/account
- Yahoo—security.yahoo.com/

GENERAL BUSINESS

While the challenges facing your targets will be quite specific to them, there are some general resources that can help you to understand more general market conditions, how businesses work, and how they fail.

- *Better: A Surgeon's Notes on Performance* by Gawande—978031 2427658
- *Good to Great: Why Some Companies Make the Leap...and Others Don't* by Collins—0066620996
- *Let's Get Real or Let's Not Play: Transforming the Buyer/Seller Relationship* by Khalsa and Illig—1591842263
- *Selling the Invisible: A Field Guide to Modern Marketing* by Beckwith—0446672319

- *SPIN Selling* by Rackham—0070511136
- *The Innovator's Solution: Creating and Sustaining Successful Growth* by Christensen and Raynor—1578518520
- *The One Thing You Need to Know: ...About Great Managing, Great Leading, and Sustained Individual Success* by Buckingham—0743261658
- *What the CEO Wants You to Know: How Your Company Really Works* by Charan—0609608398

ETHICS

While your ethics are your own, it can be quite useful to know how others expect you to act. It will vary by geographic region and by specific industry. In general, GIAC and (ISC)^2 focus on the ethical use of information in a business context. The other resources help you determine, more specifically, what ethics others might expect you to follow.

- DoD View—www.dod.mil/dodgc/defense_ethics/resource_library/resourcesindex.html
- Ethics Resource Center Ethics Toolkit—www.ethics.org/page/ethics-toolkit
- GIAC Code of Ethics—computer-forensics.sans.org/certification/ethics
- (ISC)^2 Code of Ethics—www.isc2.org/ethics/Default.aspx

Interview Questions

This is a list of interview questions in random order so you do not get stuck on any particular flow and start to expect specific questions. For practice, have a friend read you these questions so you can answer them. The goal is to run through this list enough times so that no question will take you by surprise but not so often that your response becomes scripted. Once you have eliminated the "ums" and "uhs" from your answers, you've gone far enough.

COMMON INTERVIEW QUESTIONS

- Why are you interested in this job?
- Why is there a gap in your employment history?
- What is your favorite thing about working in this industry?
- What do you most dislike about working in this industry?
- Are you good at handling pressure?
- If the job were offered to you, when could you start?
- Is there anything preventing you from working a standard shift?
- Where do you see yourself in seven years?
- Tell me about yourself.
- Describe a normal day at your current or previous job.
- Do you see yourself as a team player?
- From what sources do you get your information?
- How do you stay current in your field?
- What was the last book you read?
- What have you done in your career that you are most proud of?
- How would your coworkers describe you?
- Tell me about your strengths.
- What best motivates you?
- How do you best learn new things?
- What would you do to turn this opportunity into your dream job?
- How much are you willing to travel?
- Describe a difficult situation you experienced in the past and how you handled it.
- What was your biggest failure?

- If you had to let someone go, how would you do it?
- If you took this job, what would you wish to accomplish in the first, second, and third months?
- Tell me about a disagreement you had with a superior, peer, or direct report and how you addressed it.
- Sometimes our team has to work overtime; would that be a problem for you?
- What are some areas of improvement that previous managers have pointed out to you?
- Are you comfortable taking a leadership role, or do you prefer to be directed?
- What would you change about your current organization?
- Why do you enjoy working there?
- What was the biggest mistake that you've ever made?
- Why are you interested in working for us?
- Tell me about a time you've had to deal with an upset customer.
- What would you say were your bosses' strengths?
- What are your bosses' weaknesses?
- Tell me about your education.
- Why did you decide to talk to us about this position?
- What sort of work would you have to do to get to work early and leave late each day?
- Describe your weaknesses.
- Tell me about your leadership experiences.
- Tell me about a project that you pushed beyond the basic requirements.
- Why are you better than the other candidates?
- If this job required you to move, what would your expectations be?
- What do you like to do in your free time?
- What sort of salary do you expect?
- Do you have specific career goals?
- Tell me why I should hire you.
- Do you have any questions?

Emotional Concerns

The process described in this book is deceptively straightforward. This was a necessary trade-off, since different people require differing levels of emotional support throughout the process. To maximize understanding, the decision was made to keep this book as factual and direct as possible. The cost of this trade-off, however, is that the process appears far easier than it truly is. A certain type of person, one who is commonly found in IT and often self-identifies as an introvert, will have problems with this.

If you have never suffered from depression, issues of self-esteem, or distraction, feel free to skip this appendix. It's not written for you and you'll probably find it overly touchy-feely.

CONSTANT PROGRESS

The job search process can be debilitating. In many societies, people place high self-worth on being employed and low self-worth on being unemployed. Additionally, there is a cultural attitude of "keep your head down and do your job," where people who disrupt things get fired (or promoted for being "a straight shooter"). Thus, it is extremely common for people to wind up being laid off precisely for doing what they were told to do by their managers. This is completely unfair. Of course, if you enter into the process knowing that the system is unfair, you are in a position to take advantage of that and twist the system to meet your own ends. That's what this entire book has been about.

That said, making the system work to your advantage is easier said than done. It is unrealistic to expect you to shed a lifetime of internalized lessons after reading a single book. Thinking about some of these ideas may have been overwhelming or depressing. If that is the case, keep the following in mind:

1. There is no point in measuring yourself against anyone but you. Different people have different skills, resources, and goals. Only by

comparing yourself to who you were yesterday, last year, and last decade can you identify if you're going in the right direction.
2. A day without progress is a day lost. No one can work every minute or every hour, but most people can manage to do at least a little bit each day to advance themselves towards their goals.

To succeed, you have to keep moving forward. If you feel depressed and want to take a day off, that's okay, but only if doing so will help you keep moving over the long run. The problem is that one day off can turn into two, which can turn into three, which might as well be a week. A lost week can feed your depression and make it all the harder to get going again. So if you decide to take a day off, try very hard to just keep it to one day. Track your days off by the week or month to make sure that you're not losing too many and, more importantly, that you're not slowly increasing the number of days that you're taking off.

If you want to take a day off, try to also take half an hour at the beginning of the process to lay out what you want to accomplish the next day. By doing this, you might not make direct progress, but you've laid out a path for yourself and lowered the amount of energy it will take to get yourself moving again.

KNOWING WHEN YOU'RE STUCK

If you track your progress, you can tell when you get stuck. If you are taking off too many days compared to what you used to, you can be stuck. Be careful, though, not to measure yourself based on how many days you think you *should* be able to work. This is commonly based on how many days your friends, family, or competitors work, which violates the "don't measure yourself against others" rule.

If you are not tracking your progress—whether you never started, fell off the progress wagon, or simply felt it wasn't worth your time—there are a few other ways to identify whether you're stuck.

If you start doing research and find yourself checking email or poking around on Facebook for more than 15 minutes, you are probably avoiding a task. Odds are that that task is stuck and you've not realized it yet.

If you find yourself watching TV, playing with your kids (or pets), or reading for fun during a time you set aside to work on your job hunt, you are probably procrastinating. There is nothing wrong with having fun, of course, but if you'd rather have fun in the present than in the future, perhaps your current situation isn't bad enough to leave. You should reconsider whether you even want a different job.

If you find yourself doing absolutely nothing or spending all your time doing trivial things instead of the work you need to do, you might be depressed. Depression is common in situations like this. Unfortunately, there is nowhere near enough space to cover the specifics of living with depression. In lieu of that, use these two rules of thumb. First, if three of your friends tell you that you seem depressed or that you've been down for a while, you're depressed and should probably see someone about it. If you read the last sentence and thought that you didn't even have three friends, you are definitely depressed and should go see someone. There are many resources for dealing with depression, so find one that doesn't feel impossible but is also not entirely comfortable. That generally indicates that that approach will be different enough to help you out of the emotional trap in which you are stuck. Pause your job search until you've dealt with your emotional needs.

If you aren't certain what the next step is and, as a result, don't do anything at all, you're stuck. In this case, you need to determine where you are in the entire process and lay out a new path forward.

GETTING UNSTUCK

It often helps to think of tasks as requiring a certain amount of activation energy. In chemistry, there are processes that simply cannot happen unless enough energy has been added to a system. This is often done by heating up a solution, but it can also happen from light or a sudden shock. This energy causes the molecules to move around and form new structures, or "activate" the reaction. Catalysts can lower the amount of activation energy required to cause the reaction.

A task like "get a new job" has a huge amount of activation energy and is almost impossible for anyone but the most vivacious extroverts to approach at that level. Instead, as is done in chemistry, you can break the task down into small pieces, each requiring a smaller amount of energy. Some people can break this down into relatively small chunks and have the energy to tackle them. This can be as simple as figuring out where you want to work, getting a list of potential interviewers, building a new résumé, etc. Some people, however, need things to be smaller still. People in the middle of a depression may need the tasks to be as small as putting on pants, making coffee, and reading two pages of this book.

Wherever you are on this spectrum, the mechanism is the same. Break things down into small enough pieces to handle and make progress. Someone who works on three tiny tasks each day will soon outstrip someone who works once per month on one very large task. The key is constant forward progress.

If you're stuck, figure out why and remove what's blocking you. If you are confused by the process, reread this book and, if you're still confused, go to the Resources section and read some of the supporting books. If you're blocked by something external to the process, such as issues with your family, address them, then return to the process. If you're constrained by resources, keep working where you are or pick up a freelance gig and save up until you have enough to get you over the next level.

If you're overwhelmed by what you have to do, break things down into smaller pieces. One way to do this is to create a simple table that lists all the tasks you have to do. Then add two columns, one for what you have to do and one for when you know it's done. If you can't fill in each of those columns for each task, you have to break them down further. Here is an example:

Task	What to do?	When is it done?
Figure out what I want to do	Review lists of possible careers online and think about whether I'd like to do them.	When I've put in at least 4 but no more than 16 hours doing research and have a first, second, and third choice.
Figure out where I want to work	Research best cities to live in and best companies to work for.	When I've put in at least 8 but no more than 24 hours doing research and have a first, second, and third choice.
Find possible candidates for informational interviews	Search LinkedIn for senior-level people and directors that work for the company.	When I've put in at least 2 hours digging through LinkedIn results and have at least 10 names on the list.
Create résumé	Unknown	Unknown
Create cover letter	Write letter based on template in book.	When the letter is done and fits on one single page.
Set up appointment	Send introductory email and follow up with three phone calls.	When appointment is set, rejected, or no response to all three calls.
Create handouts	Unknown	Unknown

In this example, the "Create résumé" and "Create handouts" tasks clearly need to be broken down further. The résumé creation process could be broken apart into tasks like: "Review past timesheets," "Write story cards," and "Build résumé from story cards." The handout creation process would likely involve an industry-specific research step and possibly some brainstorming with other people in the industry.

ASKING FOR HELP

It is unrealistic to believe that you can do everything yourself. Even the creation of this book involved a copyeditor, a layout editor, a project editor, and about a dozen beta readers. It was based on the work of many others, as seen in the Resources section, and is being marketed by a large number of employees of the publisher and (hopefully) many online fans.

Anything of importance that any human has done has been assisted or influenced by others. Organizations exist because we can do more working together than we can on our own. If you want to work with an organization, you're going to need help. Reading this book is one form of help, but there are others. The hiring of a copyeditor was mentioned earlier. You may also wish to get your friends to role-play the interview with you, interview friends of friends for information on your target company or industry, or find designers to help you make your documents look good.

If you are having emotional issues that are getting in the way of you reaching your goals, you may want to talk to a therapist or job counselor. There is no weakness in seeking that sort of help, especially if they help you reach your goal faster or more easily than you otherwise would have. The end result is not the only thing that matters, but it is an important yardstick. If the people with whom you associate can help you, let them.

If your friends are getting in your way, get better friends. Friends who tell you that you can't do things, without having a discussion as to why and how you can address the weaknesses that are holding you back, are friends not worth having. They may be hanging around you to make themselves look better in comparison. They may like the feeling of control. They may just be negative people who get their happiness by making others miserable. In all these cases, what looks like help is the opposite. A therapist would be able to help you make that determination as well, as would a search on "Power and Control Wheel."

Similarly, friends who tell you that you can do anything, without considering specifics of your situation and helping you address the real barriers that get in your way, aren't good friends, either. These people tend to be self-obsessed and ignore the fact that other people have real lives with real challenges. Just saying that you can do things isn't support. Helping you find ways to do the things you want to is real support.

Once you have cut the people who harm you out of your life and added those who will help you, you should be far more ready to overcome the emotional concerns that are holding you back. This process can take a while, so address the emotional issues first; then, when you're stable, dive back into pursuing the job of your dreams.

Lightning Source UK Ltd.
Milton Keynes UK
UKOW03f1156160214

226541UK00008B/170/P